LANCASHIRE MAGIC & MYSTERY

Secrets of the Red Rose County

Kenneth Fields

Published by Sigma Leisure – an imprint of
Sigma Press, 1 South Oak Lane, Wilmslow, Cheshire SK9 6AR, England.

British Library Cataloguing in Publication Data
A CIP record for this book is available from the British Library.

ISBN: 1-85058-606-3

Typesetting and Design by: Sigma Press, Wilmslow, Cheshire.

Printed by: MFP Design & Print

Cover illustration: main picture, Colne Church (Chapter 5); smaller picture, Red Moss Head (Chapter 1)

Preface

In 1994, when I was exploring the Red Rose County for my volume *A Journey Through Lancashire*, I chanced upon many mysterious tales which I thought worthy of further investigation. At last I have now found time to return to these curious aspects of our countryside which you will find outlined in the following pages.

They are a diverse mixture which can be summed up as strange-but-true. Yet this then raises the eternal question of where truth really lies, for in our ancient landscape, where legends and pagan beliefs stretch back to prehistoric times, it is difficult to separate myth from reality. So I have distanced myself from this unending battle between sceptic and believer, merely recording tales which I feel are of great interest. Whether you believe or dispute them is, of course, a matter of personal choice.

My quest to discover this hidden face of Lancashire has led me to some fascinating sites which are visited by only a few. I have gazed on the sparkling waters of holy wells, made excursions to isolated burial mounds and stone circles, then climbed to windswept summits which still echo with memories of a half-forgotten past. I have visited Christian shrines, seen the revered relics of saints and heard of miracles which are attributed to their supernatural powers.

Constantly I have been surprised at the number of strange happenings which seem to have been recorded in every town, village and hamlet in Lancashire. And many of these are not merely legends from the distant past, but are events taking place today. For seldom a week passes without reports appearing in our newspapers that UFOs have been seen soaring across the northern sky or that ghostly apparitions are gliding through our ancient inns and old houses.

Much of the book is concerned with that obscure interface where history, religion, superstition, custom and futuristic beliefs merge. However, as well as looking at this 'unexplained' face of our county, I have also uncovered other intriguing aspects which I feel worthy of mention. These include our little-known lost villages, our rich legacy of curious landmarks, chilling tales of horrific murders and barbaric punishments, and an outline of some of the terrible disasters which have darkened our county.

Acknowledgements

A volume of this kind which embraces so many diverse topics, must by its very nature rely on the works of others. In the course of research I have consulted many ancient and some modern volumes, looked at yellowed newspaper reports, spoken to individuals, and at the end drawn my own conclusions. To all these sources, too numerous to list in detail, I extend my thanks.

Most of the sketches used as illustrations are the work of Mike Ince of Croston, to whom I am particularly grateful. I would also like to thank that highly knowledgeable local historian, John Smith of Horwich, for allowing me to use his photograph of the Red Moss Head, and Robin Smith of Bolton for supplying me with details of his research on Two Lads Hill.

Finally, as always, my special thanks go to my wife Wynne. After accompanying me to every 'mysterious' corner of the county, she had the daunting task of reading, correcting and suggesting improvements to my manuscript.

This book is dedicated to the memory of Mary Tierney of Bolton who told me many a fascinating tale from her childhood in Lancashire.

Kenneth Fields

Contents

Chapter One

Strange but True

Vanished from Blackpool

On the 5 January 1941, a twin-engined Oxford aircraft taxied down the runway at Squires Gate Airport in Blackpool and took off into the grey sky. The pilot had been warned that low cloud was shrouding the Midlands, but chose to ignore the warning. This was no inexperienced airman, nervous of the hazards of flying in bad weather, but one of the greatest aviators in history – and a woman. But sadly this was to be the last flight of Amy Johnson for she was never seen again and her final hours remain one of the great mysteries of aviation history.

Amy was a Yorkshire lass who was born in 1903, the daughter of a Hull fish merchant. A tomboy by nature, she graduated from Sheffield University in 1925 with a degree in economics, then had a number of office jobs. But later, while trying to forget a failed love affair, she began taking flying lessons, being drawn to the adventure of the sky which was the craze of the twenties. At first she seemed anything but a natural aviator, never being able to master the art of light landings. However, she persisted, finally qualifying as both a pilot and ground engineer.

Caught up in the spirit of her day, she was immediately seized with the idea of creating a flying record which would make her name. She decided to attempt the 'big one': to beat the Britain to Australia flight record which had been accomplished by Bert Hinkler in 1928 in a time of 15 days. With northern grit she went about trying to raise the capital needed for the attempt – a difficult task in a world which was in a state of economic gloom. However, never taking 'no' for an answer, she persuaded both the oil magnate Lord Wakefield and her own father of the validity of her venture. Soon she was taking to the sky in a second-hand Gipsy Moth.

With enormous confidence and almost no experience she lifted the fragile machine off the tarmac at Croydon Airport on the 5 May 1930 and headed towards Vienna. By the time she had reached Karachi the record seemed to be hers, but then bad weather prevailed for the second part of her flight. She landed exhausted in Darwin nineteen and a half days after leaving Britain. Hinkler still held the fastest time but Amy Johnson had become the first woman to complete the solo flight, and in so doing had captured the hearts of the world.

For the next decade she was seldom out of the newspaper headlines as she chased one aviation record after another, becoming the heroine that the whole world loved. She met the rich and famous, and became the subject of poems and songs. Toasted as the 'Queen of the Air' and the 'Aeroplane Girl', her name was on everyone's lips. Horatio Nicholls' popular tune of 1930 summed up the feelings of many at this time:

Amy, wonderful Amy,
How can you blame me for loving you?

In 1932 she made what at first seemed to be an ideal marriage to fellow aviator Jim Mollison, but their relationship soon turned sour. Although termed the 'Flying Sweethearts' by the press, Mollison failed to give up his other women, he had a drink problem and was bitterly jealous of the publicity which followed Amy. This became worse when she broke the England to Capetown record which Mollison himself held.

During the mid-thirties the couple attempted several joint records, Amy hoping that this would bring them closer together. But although flying solo she achieved great success, together they seemed doomed to failure. One disastrous attempt on the world long-distance flight record ended in a spectacular crash at Bridgeport in the USA. Their life together also deteriorated even further, ending in an inevitable divorce in 1938.

Towards the end of the thirties Amy had almost completely given up her pioneering flights. Her divorce, the worry her adventures caused her family and the shock of learning of the death of her friend Amelia Earhart contributed to her decision. However, flying was still her life and she needed to be fully employed, so in June 1939 she became a pilot on the Solent air ferry. This job lasted just a few months before war was declared and the company was taken over by the Air Ministry. She was now drafted into essential war work, delivering military aircraft to airfields in different parts of Britain.

On 3 January 1941 she was instructed to deliver an Oxford aircraft from Hatfield, Hertfordshire, to Prestwick in Scotland. She had then to collect another Oxford from Prestwick and fly this machine down to Kidlington airfield in Oxfordshire. Having successfully completed the first part of her mission, she flew out of Prestwick at 4 pm on Saturday, 4 January, and broke her journey by landing at Squires Gate airfield at Blackpool. In the evening she visited her sister Molly and her brother-in-law Trevor Jones who lived in Newton Drive, Blackpool. Here she spoke of a slight fault on the aircraft compass, but said lightheartedly that she would 'smell her way to Kidlington'.

On the morning of the 5 January she chatted with ground staff and RAF pilots at Squires Gate before going to her aircraft. The Duty Pilot advised her that visibility was very bad and she should consider not taking off, but she felt she could cope with the conditions. Harry Banks, a refueller at the airfield, sat with her until her take-off at 11.49 and he stated that no other person was on board.

The next official sighting of the Oxford was at 3.30 pm by a coastal convoy which was in the Thames Estuary. Several sailors reported hearing the sound of the aircraft, then they saw it spiralling overhead. Shortly afterwards they saw what they believed to be one, or perhaps two people parachuting into the sea.

HMS *Hazelmere*, in a heavy swell, sped to give assistance. Seamen threw two lines to a woman they identified floating in the water, she was wearing a flying helmet and a life-saving jacket. It seemed that she could easily have grasped the line, but she made no attempt to do so, then she disappeared beneath the stern of the vessel.

A second survivor was then seen in the water a little further away, so the Captain of the *Hazelmere*, Lt-Commander Fletcher, dived into the icy sea to attempt a rescue. He managed to reach the man and began to support him, awaiting the arrival of the lifeboat which had been launched. But the two became separated and the airman, who was wearing a flying helmet, also disappeared from view. Fletcher was rescued but was unconscious and died shortly afterwards in hospital. A later search of the area revealed two bags floating in the sea, one containing Amy Johnson's papers.

It was 1943 before she was officially declared dead, but the mystery of what happened in her final hours is still hotly debated. Like an Agatha Christie detective story there are many clues which lead to many possible solutions.

Could an aviator as experienced as Amy, who had found her way in atrocious conditions to the remotest corners of the world, have really lost her way in England? Her destination of Kidlington should have been reached

All the world loved Amy Johnson

two and a half hours before her aircraft was seen 100 miles away at the Thames Estuary, where she parachuted into the sea. Who was the other unknown man seen in the water whose rescue led to the sad death of the gallant Fletcher? And was a third man piloting the Oxford, which did not plummet directly into the sea but spiralled for several minutes?

Many theories have been put forward which claim to solve the puzzle, but still the debate goes on. Some say she had flown on a secret wartime mission to France, returning with a secret agent, which explains the second parachutist. Others say she was depressed by her divorce and committed suicide, which is why she did not grasp the line. Another solution says she merely ran out of fuel and was overcome by the icy water, and that there was no second parachutist, this was just her bag floating in the water.

In 1961 the bones of a woman were washed up on the shore at Herne Bay, which for a time raised the possibility that Amy's remains had at last been found. However, after extensive forensic investigation by the imminent scientist Dr Keith Simpson, it was conclusively established that this was not the case.

What is certain is that when that Oxford aircraft took to the misty skies above Blackpool, one of the greatest mysteries in aviation history was about to unfold.

The Beast of the Dunes

Throughout Lancashire there are pub signs which show an appealing labrador or spaniel alongside the name *Black Dog*. But these modern interpretations, by artists depicting our household pets, are far removed from the history behind many of these signs. Throughout Britain are to be found numerous legends of black dogs, which are terrifying supernatural creatures, often said to be the companion of the Devil. They are said to roam isolated wild places waiting for any passing traveller. To these unfortunates they show no mercy; a bloody and horrible death inevitably follows.

Sir Arthur Conan Doyle, whose childhood imagination was sparked by the unspoilt beauty of the Ribble Valley and the wildness of Longridge Fell, based his classic *Hound of the Baskervilles* on one such Welsh legend, but he may well have heard of Lancashire's hell hounds known as trashers or strikers. They are said to infest many parts of the county and are reputed to give vent to a horrifying scream as they pursue their terrified victims.

However, in recent years this black beast of the past seems to have reappeared for countless conflicting sightings have been claimed. Many of these describe a huge, black dog, while others say it is a cat-like creature. A black panther, a leopard or a strange wild dog has been suggested to the police by those who have caught a fleeting glance of the predator.

Although reports of this mysterious beast have been recorded for almost

A marauding killer or a supernatural beast?

two centuries, it was in early 1983 that it again caught media attention. A farmer on Exmoor reported he had lost a large number of lambs and even fully grown sheep to the marauding killer. Often all that remained of his animals were their heads, feet and skin. At first he thought that foxes or local dogs might be responsible for the loss, but later the sighting of a strange black, cat-like creature changed his mind.

A hunt, supervised by the local police, with a helicopter and fifty armed men took place, but without success. Later a detachment of highly trained marine commandos were brought in to bring down the ruthless killer, but even these failed. The beast, although seen by the soldiers, was able to avoid their bullets: it appeared to have an inherent intelligence which enabled it to keep one step ahead.

In August 1984 it seemed that the beast, or at least a similar animal, had reached Lancashire for a sighting of a cat 'as big as a lioness' had come from the Rossendale Valley. A young boy had been walking in the sunshine across Swineshaw Moor, which lies to the north of Rawtenstall and Bacup, when he suddenly came upon the beige-coloured creature leaping through a clump of rushes. He saw its huge legs and paws, and said its tail was two and a half feet long.

A local farmer substantiated the claim when he found one of his sheep had been killed nearby. It had an enormous gaping wound, its ribs having been horribly crushed by a great force, and very large paw prints could be seen in the earth. A hunt by mounted police and armed hill-farmers followed, but it seemed that the unknown beast had again escaped.

Over a decade later, in January 1997, another alarming report came in about a strange black beast that had been seen on the Lancashire coast. The police in Southport received two separate calls within half an hour concerning a 'black panther' seen at Ainsdale. Immediately a helicopter was scrambled, together with an armed response team, but again the creature escaped undetected.

When news of the sightings became public, many other people wrote to the local newspaper relating similar experiences around the coastal dunes. One man told how three years before he had met the creature in Formby Woods and other witnesses related more recent encounters in the same area. Unexplained loud growling at night, a large, black animal at least five foot long, and pets mysteriously killed, were just a few of the reports.

However, the beast of the dunes may have a supernatural explanation which is recorded in the folklore of this once isolated area. It seems the ghost dog of Formby, known as Striker, has for centuries haunted the sandhills between Ainsdale and Formby. It is said to be a large, black hound with eyes which shine in the dark, and grimly, its presence is associated with death.

Other, more rational explanations have been put forward for the numerous encounters with black beasts which continue to be recorded from all parts of Britain. Some believe they may be big cats which have either escaped from zoos, or in some cases been deliberately released by private owners who can no longer care for them.

Another theory suggests that the animal is an unknown British species which has so far completely eluded capture. In spite of our ever-growing urbanisation, its highly developed instinct guides it away from danger. But some sceptics, in spite of the evidence, remain completely unconvinced. Believing that there is no truth in it at all, their view is that people are just imagining it!

Lancashire Giants

On the 15 April 1918, in Queen's Park Hospital in Blackburn, one of England's unique characters died. Although only 29 years old, Fred Kempster – known affectionately as the 'Gentle Giant' – had become one of the best-loved celebrities of his generation.

Fred had been born in the ancient village of Avebury in Wiltshire, famous for its standing stones. Unlike other local children, he just grew and grew at an astonishing rate of four inches (10cms) a year, until it quickly became apparent that he was destined to become a giant. He eventually reached a height of eight feet four inches (2.54m) and weighed 27 stones. His thirteen feet (4m) reach enabled him to do a favourite party trick of lighting a cigarette from a gaslight in the street. With his great height came a smiling, friendly personality. He would joke with visitors, chatting about the advantages of his height, always having a kind word with the local children who loved him.

As a teenager he began working as a gardener in the nearby town of Devizes, but his fame as a giant spread throughout the country and a showman offered him a contract to go on tour. Billed as 'The World's Tallest Man', Fred soon became a favourite with the crowds who would travel long distances to see him.

His new showbusiness career took him abroad to Germany where he appeared alongside a giantess named Brunhilde who even topped his great height. Unfortunately he was still in Germany when the First World War began and he was sent to an internment camp. This seriously undermined his delicate health so that when he was eventually released, towards the end of the war, he was weak and emaciated.

Returning to his sister's home in Avebury to regain his strength, he then took to the road once more as a one-man freak show. It was while appearing at a shop in Victoria Street in Blackburn that his illness reappeared and he collapsed. It is said that eight men were needed to carry him into an ambulance and instead of using a stretcher, he was placed on a fireman's jumping sheet. When he reached Queen's Park Hospital three beds were lashed together to support him. However, despite frantic efforts by doctors, the Gentle Giant died shortly afterwards of pneumonia.

Fred had been a member of the Royal Order of Buffaloes, so ten of his fellow members carried his huge nine feet (2.7m) long coffin to his final resting place in Whalley New Road Cemetery. A special team of 14 gravediggers had been recruited to remove an estimated ten tons of earth for his grave, which measured ten feet (3m) long by three feet (1m) wide. His gravestone simply states that he was 'The British Giant'.

However, Fred Kempster is only the most recent of many giants, both real and legendary, who have lived in Lancashire. Alder and Alphin, remembered by the names of two hill summits above Saddleworth, were giants and rivals in love. The beautiful nymph, Rimmon, who lived in Chew Brook was the subject of their affection. Eventually she chose Alphin of Pots and Pans Hill to be her lover, but Alder refused to accept her decision. A furious fight followed, with great rocks being hurled from one to the other, then Rimmon watched in horror as Alphin was hit and killed. Filled with unbearable grief, she joined him in death by throwing herself from the top of a cliff. Alphin was said to have been buried near the Giant's Rock on Greenfield Moor, while the large boulders which remain along the Chew Valley testify to the giant's fight.

Another real giant, John Middleton, was born in the village of Hale near Liverpool in 1578. He grew to a height of nine feet and three inches (2.8m), and his huge hands measured seventeen inches (0.43m) across. Curiosity brought many visitors to see him, and he became something of a local celebrity. Then Sir Gilbert Ireland of Hale Hall, knowing that King James had a liking for giants and dwarfs, persuaded him to go to London.

Dressed in a fine doublet of white and red, with flowered breeches and green stockings, he looked magnificent when he arrived at the Royal Court. Soon it was arranged that he would fight the King's champion, whom he beat quite effortlessly, winning a prize of twenty pounds. On his way home he called at Oxford University where students from Lancashire gave him a lavish welcome. Before he departed his portrait was painted so that it could be hung with pride in the library of Brasenose College as a record of his visit.

John Middleton died in 1643 at the age of 65, and his grave can be seen in St Mary's churchyard in Hale. The cottage where he was born still stands and he is remembered as The Child of Hale in the local inn sign. His huge effigy has also been skilfully carved by two Merseyside artists from the trunk of a beech tree.

However, John Middleton was only following the lead of another Lancashire giant when he made his journey to London, but surprisingly this was a woman. During the reign of Henry VIII, a girl of great height, who became known as Westminster Meg, left her native county to join the army. Starting off in the manner she intended to continue, on arriving in the capital she mercilessly beat up the carrier for charging her too much.

She went on to have a distinguished career in the army, seeing service in France, which resulted in her receiving a well-deserved pension. Her exploits became legendary, catching the imagination of many writers of the time. She became immortalised by both a proverb which was popular in the 17th century – 'as long as Meg of Westminster' – and by a ballad written by Ben Jonson:

Westminster Meg,
With her long leg,
As long as a crane,
And feet like a plane,
With a pair of heels,
As broad as two wheels.

According to Arthurian tradition, it was in Manchester that the great Saxon giant, Sir Tarquin, lived. He was a cruel and treacherous man who showed no mercy to his foes having taken the fortress from its rightful owners. However, the valiant knight Sir Lancelot of the Lake was determined to rid the county of the evil monster. A confrontation eventually came, bringing a furious sword fight between the two enemies which ended only when the giant was decapitated.

Richard Formby, who lived during the late 14th century, was a Lancashire giant who came from a wealthy background, his family home being Formby Hall at Formby. He grew to a great height, which made him ideal for the position he held in the royal court as armour-bearer to the Lancastrian kings.

Following his death in 1407 he was buried in York Minister, then almost forgotten for over four centuries. But in 1829 a mad man named Jonathan Martin deliberately set fire to the choir stalls, causing considerable damage. A burning beam, which fell from the roof, landed on the gravestone of Richard Formby causing it to crack and exposing his bones. These were later measured and his height was verified as seven feet (2.1m). His cracked gravestone was then brought back to St Luke's church in Formby where it remains.

Spring-heeled Jack

One of the great unresolved mysteries of England, which spanned more than a century, concerns the strange leaping giant who became known in Victorian newspapers as spring-heeled Jack. This weird creature, who made an appearance in both Everton and Warrington, has fascinated people ever since. Was he an alien who somehow became marooned on earth? Perhaps a deformed man born with extraordinary powers? Or maybe the whole affair was an elaborate hoax which caught the public imagination, then became perpetuated by successive generations?

It was in London in 1837, the same year that Queen Victoria came to the throne, that spring-heeled Jack made his first appearance. A man who was walking home from work across isolated Barnes Common was suddenly confronted by a weird figure which leapt with astonishing agility over the railings of a cemetery. Fearful, the man looked straight into the face of the strange leaper who had round, glowing eyes, pointed ears and a large, sharp nose. Luckily the man was able to escape, but three girls who met spring-heeled Jack in the same area the next day were not so lucky. This time he attacked the terrified trio, ripping at their clothes and leaving one girl unconscious.

Over the next few months several other reports of the antics of spring-heeled Jack hit the headlines. He attacked a servant girl named Mary Stevens as she walked near Clapham Common, then he assaulted two sisters, Lucy and Margaret Scales, at Limehouse. They were saved by their brother and the weird, cloaked creature made its escape by leaping over a 14 feet (4.3m) high wall.

But the best description came from 25-year-old Jane Alsop who heard loud knocking on the door of her home in Bow. The tall, shadowy figure hidden by the gloom said he was a policeman who had captured spring-heeled Jack. When Jane brought a candle its yellow flame revealed not a policeman, but the hideous face of Jack himself. His eyes stared at her like balls of fire, then suddenly blue and white gas spurted from his mouth, which almost blinded her. In the turmoil that followed he began to tear at her clothes with his claw-like hands, but luckily her screams brought her father and sister to her aid, causing Jack to make a hasty retreat.

In 1838 a man from Peckham wrote to Sir John Cowan, the Lord Mayor of London, telling him how he had witnessed the incredible leaping creature. His letter was read out during a Mansion House meeting, finally opening the official debate on spring-heeled Jack which was destined to continue for decades. Scores of other sightings now followed, including one from a servant boy who told how the creature knocked on the door of his master's house, off Commercial Road. The terrified boy managed to escape from wild-eyed Jack, but noticed that a coat of arms together with the letter 'W' was prominent beneath Jack's cloak. This led some to speculate that a well-known hoaxer of the day, the Marquess of Waterford, might be responsible

Mysterious Spring-heeled Jack

for the antics. However, twenty years later this was discounted when the marquess died, but spring-heeled Jack continued to flourish.

Such was the publicity now surrounding his exploits that even the hero of Waterloo, the Duke of Wellington, attempted to capture him, but sadly with no success. Jack was now moving out of London, reports of his movements suggested he was spreading his wings. In 1855, following a deep snowfall, his footprints were found running over miles of the Devon countryside. In 1877 two army guards shot at him at point blank range when he failed to halt at the entrance to Aldershot barracks. But their bullets had no effect, he leapt casually away, leaving them convinced he was immortal.

Over the next few years he was seen in Shropshire and Lincolnshire, displaying the amazing athletic ability which never failed to astonish all who saw him. Then in September 1904 he arrived in Lancashire, giving the people of Everton a taste of his gravity-defying performance. Crowds watched open-mouthed as he sprang across the rooftops, then later he was seen clinging to the steeple of St Francis Xavier's Church. He hurled himself to the floor, which would have been the end of any normal man, but not spring-heeled Jack. With tenacious defiance he looked down on the screaming crowd who could only stare in disbelief as he flew effortlessly over the rooftops of William Henry Street, then out of the headlines for another sixteen years.

His next appearance came at Warrington in 1920 when more crowds witnessed him leaping from street level up to the very top of the houses in playful fashion, before disappearing over the top of the railway station. The last report of his whereabouts may well have been at Monmouth in 1948, when a weird man answering his description was seen bounding over a stream.

With the coming of the age of space travel some have compared spring-heeled Jack to an astronaut, for some reports say he wore a transparent helmet and similar clothing. His strange, glowing eyes, his ability to leap astonishing distances, and his fiery breath have also convinced others that he was not from our planet. But sadly, as it is now half a century since he made his last appearance, we are unlikely to ever know the astonishing truth.

A Mummified Head

Sitting on a circular black base where her young body once stood, the remarkable Red Moss mummified head at first glance seems to be quite grotesque. A partially opened jaw reveals her uneven, blackened teeth, the end of what was once perhaps a noble nose has long since disappeared and sad, deep hollows sink down were sparkling eyes looked out. Yet after overcoming the initial shock of first seeing this 2000-year-old human head, a feeling of horror is quickly replaced with one of sympathy. For these are the mortal remains of a fifteen-year-old girl who would have looked, acted and had all the appeal of girls of her age. Yet instead of growing into womanhood and having a husband and children of her own, her tribe chose a different fate for her. She was to suffer a terrible sacrificial death, now followed by the indignity of having her mummified head displayed.

Red Moss is a low-lying wetland area which lies on the outskirts of Horwich, close to the new football stadium recently built for Bolton Wanderers. A feature of this site of special scientific interest is the high quality peat which for over a century has been removed by skilled peat-cutters. Many of these men had their family roots in Holland where for generations the art of quickly removing the rich black peat was perfected.

It was during the last war, in November 1943, that one of these peat-cutters was horrified to find the blackened head staring out at him from the watery earth. His first thoughts were that a murder had been committed with the body being hidden in the peat, so the police were immediately informed. The find could not have happened at a more unfortunate time for the local constabulary: not only were they undermanned due to the war, but it was the day of their great social event, the Policeman's Ball. However, this could not stand in the way of a possible murder investigation, which was thankfully a rare event at the time, so an investigation was quickly launched. The area of the find was cordoned off, forensic experts were summoned and the police, instead of dancing around a warm ballroom, were spending a cold November night on Red Moss.

When the experts eventually announced that the remains were certainly human but not recent, being many centuries old, a sigh of relief echoed around Horwich Police Station. The mummified head was taken away for further examination, and in the wartime atmosphere which prevailed when every day brought a different crisis, it was soon forgotten. Remarkably it was to be over fifty years before it was rediscovered.

In the 1990s when Bolton Council began considering Red Moss as a possible site for the creation of a huge waste tip, many local voices were raised in opposition. The Red Moss Action Committee was established with the aim of fighting the proposals and preserving the precious peat moss habitat. One of its members, dentist Dr Nigel Entwistle, then heard about the almost forgotten mummified head; a find which emphasised the archaeological importance of the site. With great determination he decided to track it down. In 1996 the trail eventually ended at the Anatomy Department of Birmingham University where the head had been kept for half a century.

It seems that the colourful Celtic people who lived in this part of Lancashire during the first century, probably chose this unfortunate 15-year-old girl as a human sacrifice. We can only guess at their motives and the strange religious rituals that accompanied the death of this sacrificial virgin. Perhaps they were pleading with their gods to rid their homeland, Brigantia, of the Roman invaders who were threatening their very existence.

After the mummified head has been fully examined by Manchester University, who consider it to be one of the best preserved specimens of its type in Britain, it will probably be displayed in Bolton Museum. And although 2000 years ago it failed to repel the might of Rome, in 1996 it helped to sway the argument against creating a waste tip at Red Moss, hopefully preserving a Celtic sacred site forever.

Buried Treasure

The dream of acquiring wealth through the discovery of hidden treasure has occupied many literary minds in the past for in an age when no bank vaults existed, often the only safe place to keep money was deep in a hole in the ground. Of course, there was then always the risk of unexpected death occurring before the hiding place could be revealed – an event which has been the basis of many legends. This has led in recent years, with the availability of metal detectors, to treasure hunting becoming a popular activity. However, would-be seekers of instant wealth ought to be aware that much of the treasure reputedly hidden in Lancashire is guarded by supernatural forces!

One of these hidden treasures is said to lie on the site of Hulme Hall, an ancient house which was demolished last century. Originally it was the home of the Prestwich family, then it was sold in 1660 to Sir Oswald Mosley. The Mosley treasure was hidden in the estate by the Lady dowager, who protected it with a series of occult incantations. Unfortunately, the old lady suddenly fell ill then died before she could reveal the hiding place to her son.

A thorough search was made of the house and grounds immediately following her death, but the treasure was not found, forcing her son to live in near poverty. Over the centuries many other attempts have been made to find the hoard, even using astrologers and fortune-tellers, but none have brought success. The hall was eventually sold to the Duke of Bridgewater who razed it to the ground, but still no treasure was discovered amongst the rubble.

A chance discovery in 1840 revealed one of England's most fascinating treasure hoards. It happened when workmen were repairing the banks of the River Ribble at Cuerdale near Preston, following damage caused by a strong gale. During the operation they dug up a wooden chest which was lined with lead. Breaking it open they were astonished to find ten thousand gleaming silver coins together with a thousand ounces of silver ingots.

Most of the coins were Danish, having been minted at York by the Kings of Northumbria. The rest of the hoard was made up of English coins from the time of Alfred the Great and Edward the Elder, together with a number of continental coins. It is now thought that the hoard had been buried by Viking warriors who were on the retreat during the early 10th century. The coins were marvellously preserved, and some are now on permanent display at the Harris Museum in Preston.

Another treasure hoard uncovered by supernatural forces was associated with Syke's Lumb Farm, an ancient building which lay at Mellor Brook close to the Ribble. Here, during the turmoil of the War of the Roses, lived a childless couple who were the last of their line. They had managed to acquire a considerable fortune, but the old man was in poor health and his wife was afraid of being attacked by the marauding bands of soldiers. So to ease her mind they decided to hide the treasure by placing it in earthenware pots, then burying it beneath the roots of an apple tree in their orchard.

Fortunately, the war came to an end without any trouble at the farm, but by this time the ailing old man had died leaving his wife alone in the house. Shortly afterwards she too died, her end coming so quickly that she was not able to divulge the secret hiding place. Her relatives searched for the fortune without success, then as the years passed the memory of its existence grew dim. But Syke's wife, even in death, had not forgotten for her spirit could not rest with the secret: her ghost was often being seen gliding restlessly along the local lanes.

Many years later the owner of the farm, having been drinking heavily, saw the ghost in the orchard. Full of false courage he approached it, asking why it haunted the spot. The apparition did not answer, but instead led him to the decayed stump of an old tree. He later began to dig up the land and in a short time, to his amazement, uncovered the buried treasure. The ghost of Syke's wife then appeared for the last time, her wrinkled face bearing a broad grin.

In 1961 council workmen were uprooting an old sycamore tree in Beauclerk Gardens in St Anne's, when about thirty inches (0.76m) below ground level they found a small chamber pot. Inside was a hoard of 383 coins which dated from 1550 to 1643. It is believed they were probably hidden about 1645, during the turmoil of the Civil War. Being in a poor state of preservation, they required cleaning using ultra sound, and at an inquest they were later declared to be treasure trove.

At Clitheroe in 1755 a hoard of nearly one thousand Roman coins were found on the line of a Roman road, and a century later, at Formby, nineteen coins dating from the 17th century were found hidden in the thatch of an old house. Finally, in 1991 at Holly House Farm at Parbold, a joiner who was renovating the building discovered a Cromwellian rapier in the loft. It had lain undiscovered for an incredible three hundred years.

So it seems that the romance of finding a hidden fortune has not died, even if in some cases the help of unearthly guardians is required!

The Devil's Highway

Although many of our traditional superstitions relating to certain numbers have been inherited from our pagan forefathers, the number 666, known as the Devil's Number, is derived from the New Testament book of Revelation. This was written about AD90 when Christians were being persecuted for their beliefs, for at this time in the Roman Empire it was mandatory to worship the Emperor.

The book of Revelation was written by John and it discloses a series of hidden messages of inspiration to those being persecuted, but in a vivid symbolic language. This would have been widely understood by the Christians of the period, but not the Roman authorities who could have used suspicious letters as evidence for further persecution.

The symbolic writings outline with powerful imagery the total defeat of evil, seen as Satan or the Devil, by Christ. Dominating many of the tales is the number seven, which is known as God's Number. These include the seven churches, the scroll with seven seals, the seven trumpets and the seven bowls of God's anger.

It is in Revelation 13, known as the Two Beasts, that the Devil's Number is given. The Two Beasts of this symbolic tale are the Roman Empire and Emperor Worship, which represent the Anti-Christ. But the message to Christians is that every age will bring forward an equivalent enemy who will need to be overcome. The final verses state:

'The beast forced all the people, small and great, rich and poor, slave and free, to have a mark placed on their right hands and foreheads. No one could buy or sell unless he had this mark, that is, the beast's name or the number that stands for the name.

This calls for wisdom. Whoever is intelligent can work out the meaning of the number of the beast, because the number stands for a man's name. Its number is 666.'

Over the years many scholars have interpreted this message in different ways, trying out codes to actually come up with the name of an individual of the period, Nero Caesar being the likely candidate. Others believe it is linked with God's Number 7, meaning that however many times the beast's Number 6 is repeated, it will never be as powerful as God.

This symbolic number from Revelations is still believed by some to be unlucky, those of a superstitious nature taking care to avoid it. This was publicised in 1990 when the Driver and Vehicle Licensing Centre at Swansea took the decision to remove the digits 666 from their computerised car number plate system. Although refusing to acknowledge any supernatural connection, following many complaints from drivers the change was made. They also agreed to change any existing registrations which had the 'Devil's Number'.

In Lancashire it is what has become known as the Devil's Highway which

A warning sign on the 'Devil's Highway' near Darwen

has gained an infamous reputation, for along this road many strange and tragic incidents have been recorded. Classified as the A666, it starts at Pendlebury on the fringe of Manchester, where it leaves the main A6. It passes through Bolton, Darwen and Blackburn, finally ending at Langho near Whalley, where it joins the A59.

But it is along St Peter's Way, which is just a mile-and-a-half long section of the road between Farnworth and Bolton, that many tragedies have occurred. Over a period of ten years, 12 people are known to have attempted suicide by jumping off bridges above the highway, and in 1990 a man suffered terrible injuries when he was pushed over the parapet of a bridge by another man who was later charged with attempted murder. The problem had become so acute that engineers were considering erecting anti-climb screens along the bridges.

People have also claimed to have seen weird, moving shadows along the road, and many accidents and minor mishaps have occurred. A section of the highway had to be closed when an unknown mine shaft was discovered, then shortly afterwards workmen fractured a gas main at Kearsley, putting the town on red alert. One local man also believes that many families who live along the road have experienced more than their fair share of personal misfortunes.

One of the strangest effects reported by some people travelling along the Devil's Highway is that of time loss, when they remember nothing of their journey. One market worker told how he and a colleague took an unexplained half hour longer than was normal on the short car trip from Bolton to Pendlebury. They arrived at their destination dazed and distressed, unable to recollect what had happened along the way. 'It is just as though we had vanished off the face of the earth," he later recalled.

In April 1997 it was widely reported that Bev Callard, popular star of Coronation Street, had an extremely lucky escape when her sports car went out of control on the A666 near Bolton. On a dry, straight section of the highway, at just 40 mph, the four month old Alfa suddenly veered into crash barriers. Although badly shaken, suffering from bruising and whiplash, the actress was not seriously hurt, but her car was battered and had to be towed away.

Another section of the A666, between Egerton and Darwen, has also become a notorious accident zone. Wreaths line the moorland roadside where so many have tragically lost their lives, and special signs have been erected to warn of the danger.

Chapter Two

Mysterious Happenings

Lost Singleton Thorpe

Most of us accept the present face of Lancashire without question, being familiar with many of its cities, towns and villages. Yet few of us realise that much of it has been created by chance happenings rather than by careful planning. It is fascinating to realise that by a twist of fate our county could have grown in an entirely different way. During Roman times both Manchester and Ribchester were important military garrisons built on the side of rivers. Yet today one has become a huge, sprawling city of international renown, while the other remains a sleepy village surrounded by the unspoilt beauty of the Ribble Valley. Each town has a different tale to tell, many having seen a rapid expansion from rural obscurity during the heady days of the Industrial Revolution. This often resulted from the personal thrust for power of local capitalists who, seizing the opportunity, created the factory system which transformed our landscape. However, there are other, almost forgotten, Lancashire villages that have now completely disappeared from our maps.

Few of the thousands of annual visitors who each year flock to Blackpool are aware that the remains of a lost village lies just off the Fylde coast. Its sad story was told around local firesides for generations before being written down by the Revd William Thornber in his *History of Blackpool* in the 1840s.

This coastline, which to the casual observer appears permanent, is, in fact, constantly changing. It is said that during the 16th century its boundary of sandhills lay much further to the west and contained the village of Singleton Thorpe. Protected by oak trees, the village was linked by road to the Wyre estuary near the present day Fleetwood. Its inhabitants made their living both as farmers and fishermen, and the local pub, The Penny Stone Inn, provided welcome accommodation for travellers who enjoyed its famous penny pints of ale. The inn had derived its name from a huge rock which lay close to the hostelry door; this formed part of a stone circle known as Carlin and the Colts. The innkeeper had inserted a metal ring into what had become known as the Penny Stone, where the customers could tether their horses.

The end of Singleton Thorpe fulfilled a prophecy because it had been said that its doom was linked to that of a foreign power's thwarted ambitions. This turned out to be Drake's famous victory over the Spanish Armada, when the scurrying vessels were forced to retreat northwards. On the 29th July 1588 a huge storm swept across the Irish sea, scattering the ships and threatening the villagers of Singleton Thorpe. Many fled inland to escape the battering waves of a sea which failed to ebb, but instead flowed twice in 12 hours. A massive tidal wave struck the final blow, destroying the inn and all the houses, drowning the few villagers who remained, and permanently altering the boundary of the coastline.

Those villagers who were fortunate enough to escape established themselves many miles from the sea, at the present village of Singleton. Three hundred years later, towards the end of the last century, curious locals searched the sands to see if they could find evidence of the lost village. A mile west of Norbreck they discovered the tops of trees, a lintel and doorpost, and the foundations of a wall. Others say they have heard ghostly voices and the laughter of revellers carried by the wind across the waves from the submerged Penny Stone Inn!

Another casualty of the same horrific storm was a Spanish galleon which was beached near Rossall Grange. A band of local men attempted to board the stricken vessel but were driven back by cannon and musket fire. Eventually the rising tide allowed the ship to make its escape, its determined gunners firing two parting shots. It is said that these two cannon balls were discovered in the 17th century when the old building was demolished, and they are now kept at Rossall School which stands close to the site.

Other Vanished Villages

Singleton Thorpe is not the only coastal village to have disappeared from the map of Lancashire for this once treacherous lowland area, which stretches from the Mersey to Morecambe Bay, fought a constant battle with the sea. Shifting sandhills piled high by the tides gave way to marsh land, known locally as mosses, which contained a host of shallow meres. South of the Ribble the largest of these, Martin Mere, was about three miles long and two miles wide, and was finally drained in 1813. Others, including Rainford Moss, Halsall Moss, Chat Moss and Red Moss, spread inland towards the rising Pennine hills. North of the Ribble, the Fylde was equally marshy, with Marton Mere and the mosses of Rawcliffe, Stalmine and Pilling not being drained until the 1830s.

When the Romans first attempted to chart Lancashire's wild coast during the 2nd century, their cartographer, Ptolemy, named what is assumed to be the Ribble estuary, as Belisama. At this time the river appears to have poured into the sea further south, close to present day Southport, and our familiar Mersey estuary was a large marsh. But the exact location of the Roman port of Portus Sentantiorum remains a mystery. Some believe it, too, was a victim of the shifting coastline, which today is marked by a bank of brown sand that can be seen at low tide off the coast at Knott End.

Birkdale, which means the birch-tree valley, is all that remains of the lost township of Argarmeols. This was in existence during the early Norman period but is believed to have been washed away by the sea in the late 14th century. Otho de Halsall, who is known to have held land at Argarmeles in 1361, pleaded at the time that it had been 'annihilate by the sea'. By the 16th century its existence was just an ancient story in the minds of old men.

Freshfield, which lies near Formby, is a new village which replaced an older settlement that was also buried by the sand. Originally named Church Mere, it disappeared between 1750 and 1850, but was then reclaimed by a Mr Fresh who covered the sand with soil. Not far away, off Formby Point, lay a deep channel with a thriving port, but this too had completely vanished by 1750, being lost to the sea.

But if it was nature that brought to an end many of these coastal settlements, further inland it was the hand of man. This resulted from the rapid population expansion of many Lancashire towns during the Industrial Revolution, which brought with it the pressing need for drinking water. The folly of not providing basic sanitation was highlighted when even the royal family was proved not to be immune from the spread of disease when, in 1861, Prince Albert died from typhoid.

This necessity to provide clean drinking water resulted in many reservoirs being built in secluded Pennine valleys, but there was a price to pay by the local population. Often it was just a single farm or cottage which lay in the path of the new development, but sometimes it was a complete community. In 1925 the Fylde Water Board began to construct Stocks Reservoir near Slaidburn, in the lovely Hodder Valley. This scheme to provide much needed water for Blackpool, sadly brought to an end the ancient village of Stocks-in-Bowland, also known as Dalehead. Twenty cottages, a post office and shop, a church, a vicarage and a school were all lost. The villagers, who mainly moved into Slaidburn, could only watch as their former homes disappeared under the water. Only their church, now rebuilt on a lonely high point, remains as a poignant reminder of a lost community.

Watergrove village near Rochdale suffered a similar fate in the 1930s. Over two hundred people lived in the village which consisted of over forty houses, two mills, a chapel and two pubs. They all had to vacate their homes, which are now covered by the grey waters of what was named the Watergrove Reservoir. A trail meanders around the perimeter of the site, with a sad reminder of the former village present in the History Wall. Here datestones, mullion windows and an ancient animal drinking trough have been preserved from the lost buildings.

The West Pennine Moors, one of Lancashire's most popular beauty spots, has many reminders of lost communities. At its north-eastern corner lies Haslingden Grane, a sweeping moorland valley which lies in the shadow of the high hills. At the beginning of the last century it was inhabited by a thriving community of around 1300 people. Known as Graners, they lived in farms and hamlets, earning their living as farmers, weavers and quarry workers. In the valley there were three mills, a church, chapel, pub and a school. But when Calf Hey Reservoir was built in the valley in 1859, followed by Ogden Reservoirs in 1912, a conflict of interests arose. It was considered that the risk of pollution to the water supply was too high so the residents were encouraged to leave. Slowly Haslingden Grane became depopulated, a process which was complete by about 1926 when the church of St Stephen was demolished and rebuilt at the end of the valley. Today the tumbled ruins of cottages which lie half-hidden in the moorland grass are sad reminders of the lost village.

Anglezarke Moor, with its windswept ridges and peaty summits, is a magnet for hillwalkers who wish to experience the wildness of the West Pennines. But as they penetrate deep into the lonely valleys which cross the moor they find a host of ruined farmhouses which show that once these uplands were well-populated. Drinkwaters, Old Rachel's, Parson's Bullough and Higher Hempshaw's are some of the picturesque names of isolated dwellings that have now disappeared. In the 14th century the part of this community which overlooked the infant River Yarrow was the hamlet of Elmshaw, which had become known as Helmshawsyde in 1520.

It was a combination of the building of the Rivington Reservoirs and the availability of less demanding work that brought about the depopulation of this moor. In 1847 an Act of Parliament had given Liverpool Corporation authority to embark on the most advanced waterworks scheme in the world. Over the next twenty years four large reservoirs had been constructed at Rivington and two near Abbey Village, together with six filter beds. Several farms and houses lay directly in the path of the scheme, together with the ancient Black-a-Moor's Head Inn at Rivington, all of which were eventually demolished.

These uplands were the main catchment area for the new reservoirs. So again, as at Haslingden Grane, the possibility of water contamination needed to be minimised so the residents were encouraged to leave. Some were probably happy to vacate the hostile moorland, finding an easier living in the cotton mills or the prestigious new locomotive works at Horwich, but others who had prosperous farms were more reluctant to give up a way of life their families had known for centuries. But by the end of the First World War the last homestead had been vacated, the empty farms were then left to become victims of the Pennine weather.

Lovely Wycoller, however, which sits in an idyllic moorland valley near Colne, is a vanished village which has miraculously been re-born. A tranquil beck meanders through its centre, crossed by an ancient packhorse bridge which leads to the ruins of 16th-century Wycoller Hall, the former home of the Cunliffe family. This building was familiar to Charlotte Brontë who immortalised it as Ferndean Manor in her novel *Jane Eyre*. It was occupied until 1818 when, following the death of the last squire who was heavily in debt,

Ruined Wycoller Hall

the hall and lands were sold. Standing alone and neglected, the once proud building slowly became the victim of time, losing its roof and falling into a sad ruin.

The windswept uplands around Wycoller had been home to Bronze Age man, then later the Anglo-Saxons found the sheltered valley an ideal place in which to raise their cattle and sheep. By the late 15th century, handloom weaving had become established in cottages and farms, which later led to a thriving local industry centred on the old hall. Sadly, this came to an abrupt end with the coming of the Industrial Revolution, when the handlooms could no longer compete with the power-driven mills of Nelson and Colne. By 1870 Wycoller had become almost a ghost village, its former residents having been forced to leave to find work in the towns. Like its ancient hall, the cottages which stand alongside the beck, began to tumble. It seemed that the forlorn village was doomed to disappear completely.

However, during the early forties a forward-looking group of local people who were concerned about the decline of the valley had a meeting. This led to the Friends of Wycoller being formed and three decades of campaigning to save the village. In 1973 this finally paid off when Lancashire County Council purchased the village and the surrounding land. Since then an amazing transformation has taken place, with the village becoming the nucleus of a Country Park. The once derelict cottages are now occupied by permanent residents, and an Information Centre and a Hill Study Centre have been created, making Wycoller a unique success story.

Lancashire Ley Lines

Of the many earth mysteries which surround us, ley lines or leys are perhaps the most intriguing for their existence raises all manner of fascinating questions about our prehistoric ancestors. From early in the last century, many local historians became increasingly interested in prehistoric sites in Britain. Several of these dedicated men, after a lifetime of study, came to believe that these ancient earthworks were linked to each other along invisible straight lines. It was not, however, until 1920 that an amateur archaeologist named Alfred Watkins gave widespread publicity to the fascinating theory. He termed these lines "leys" because he discovered that many of them intersected close to towns and villages with names which contained the word "ley". "Ley" was an Anglo-Saxon term meaning "forest clearing".

Alfred Watkins was born in Hereford in 1855, where as a young man he worked as a brewer's representative. His job took him deep into the English countryside and across the Welsh border, where he became absorbed by the ancient customs and legends which were a rich part of the local culture. This led him to a lifelong interest in all aspects of our history, particularly enjoying visits to ancient sites, which he often photographed. He became a keen photographer in his youth, when photography was in its infancy, and became both the inventor and manufacturer of several pieces of photographic equipment.

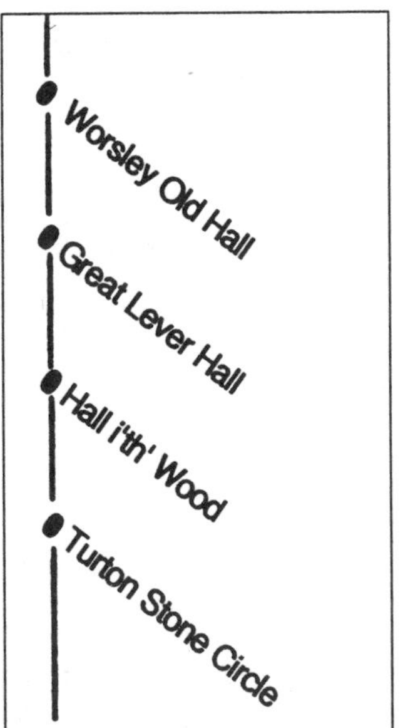

One of Lancashire's first recorded Ley Lines

In 1920, when Watkins was sixty-five years old, his knowledge and observations of prehistoric sites led to him becoming ever more convinced of the truth of the ley theory. He pored over maps then he made field trips to such places as burial mounds, churches, stone circles, hill forts, and holy wells, which he believed were aligned in a way that was more than coincidental. His thoughts were first publicly put forward in his booklet *Early British Trackways* (1922), then expanded in his well-known volume *The Old Straight Track* (1925).

Watkins' theory was greeted with great scepticism by some professional archaeologists of his day, but in spite of this his work created a great deal of general interest. People all over the country became absorbed by 'ley hunting', forming a Straight Track Club whose members became dedicated to discover new leys. But following Watkins' death in 1935, interest began to dwindle; his book went out of print and then World War II effectively brought ley hunting to an end. However, during the fifties a revival of interest in the subject began which still continues today. Earth mysteries had caught the public's imagination and *The Old Straight Track* was rediscovered. Alfred Watkins was now hailed by many to have been a visionary who, alone, had recognised an intriguing feature of our history that so many had missed.

What still remains a mystery, however, is the purpose of this strange alignment of seemingly unconnected sites? This question has led to many answers, ranging from the scientific to the bizarre. Watkins believed that they were prehistoric trade routes, but others say they are hidden lines of unexplained earth energy, sometimes detectable by dowsing. Ufologists have suggested that UFO activity is greater along leys, so they are really hidden flight lanes, but others believe they are connected with ancient religious beliefs. So the unsolved mystery of leys continues, seldom taken seriously by the professional archaeologist, but fascinating to many others.

In *The Old Straight Track* Watkins recorded three Lancashire leys which had been identified by Harold A Barnes of Farnworth. The first connected Worsley Old Hall, Great Lever Hall, Hall i' th' Wood and a Druidical Circle (Turton Heights); the second linked Wardley Hall, Kenyon Peel Hall, Hulton Park, a conical hill in Haigh Hall Park, Wrightington Hall and a tumulus; and the third aligned Blackrod Church, Leyland Park, Hindley Church, a tumulus, Myddleton Hall and Latchford Church.

Since that time, with the introduction of more detailed Ordnance Survey maps, ley hunting has been made easier. Other Lancashire leys have been discovered, but care has to be taken when aligning sites to eliminate mathematical coincidence. It is accepted by many that a ley must be a straight line which aligns at least four sites over a distance of just a few miles, although some ley hunters are of the opinion that the ley should align five sites within a ten-mile length.

It is believed that the network was created between 2600BC and 5000BC, so the sites to look for should date from this period. However, more recent buildings such as churches and castles are found on leys, for these were often built on pagan or strategic sites which are much older than the present structures. A place name may also indicate where ancient landmarks once existed even if there is now no apparent prehistoric site. So for a ley to be really proven, local historical research needs to be carried out, and the ley walked along to discover, perhaps, ancient features which are not apparent on a map.

Another feature of our hidden landscape which has also aroused interest in recent years is the discovery of Zodiac patterns. It began in 1929 when Katherine Maltwood, an artist and sculptor, was illustrating a map for a book on the Holy Grail. Poring over the Ordnance Survey map of Glastonbury in Somerset, where King Arthur is reputedly buried, an odd aspect of the landscape took her eye. She noticed that a curve of the river, together with other features of the countryside such as hedgerow boundaries and footpaths, linked up to form the shape of a lion. Further research eventually revealed that a complete Glastonbury Zodiac could be traced by linking up similar sites.

Since that time several Zodiacs and other figures have been discovered, including at least two in Lancashire: the Pendle Zodiac which spreads out from Pendle Hill, and the Lamanche which takes it name from La(ncashire), Man(chester) and Che(shire).

Crop Circles

In July 1990 at Lowton, near Leigh, a strange circle of flattened corn appeared overnight in a field at Sandup Farm. This, one of the first reports of a crop circle in Lancashire, naturally caused a great deal of speculation. Immediately a local ufologist declared it to be part of a national network of such circles which he believes act as guides to UFOs, while a sceptical farmer said it was a deliberate hoax, created by 'youngsters on motorbikes'. So, typical of such events, the battle lines were once more drawn between the staunch believers in 'mysterious happenings' and those who are convinced of a more rational explanation.

The recent origin of what have become known as crop circles can be traced to 1980 when their existence was first widely publicised. Circles of flattened oats were reported at Westbury in Wiltshire, close to the town of Warminster which has long been associated with UFO activity. There have been similar reports from many other parts of the world, and now there are indications that the phenomenon is not entirely new: several reports from the past seem to indicate that isolated crop circles have, indeed, appeared, including one in Kent in 1918.

The publicity which has followed the appearance of so many crop circles has naturally raised the question of how they are formed. Even after many years of study, 'cereologists' are still divided into different camps: one group believes that crop circles are formed by paranormal forces, another group says that they are man-made hoaxes, while the scientific believe they are produced by whirlwinds known as a plasma-vortexes. That many of the crop circles have been produced by hoaxers has now been proved beyond doubt for in some cases the deception has been readily admitted.

However, although well aware of the work of tricksters, some people are convinced that crop circles can be produced by natural forces. One of the most interesting scientific explanations, known as the Plasma-Vortex theory, says a vortex or mini-whirlwind is formed when a gust of wind is obstructed by a hill. This spinning air then meets still air on the leeward side of the hill, producing an invisible spiralling column which also draws in electricity from the atmosphere. This static electricity, which makes a high-pitched noise, is forced downward by the vortex towards the ground. If a cereal crop is in the field the action of the spiral flattens it down, forming a crop circle.

Although a team of Japanese scientists have produced a crop circle in this way under laboratory conditions and a Guildford couple actually witnessed one being created as they walked alongside a corn field, the sceptics and the mystical believers are still not convinced. For them it is still either hoaxers or UFOs which are undoubtedly responsible for these fascinating patterns.

UFOs in the Sky

In recent years tales of UFOs have become commonplace, seldom a week passes without someone seeing unexplained lights in the sky. But this is nothing new; man has always been obsessed with the heavens. In 1254 monks at St Albans saw 'a kind of ship' in the sky and in 1290 the Abbot of Byland Abbey in Yorkshire saw another silver disc. Sightings of unexplained objects were later recorded in a book published in 1646 entitled *Strange Signes from Heaven*. These continued through the 18th and 19th centuries with many eminent men writing about mysterious lights they had seen, including the president of the Royal Society and a well-known Greenwich astronomer.

But modern interest in the subject intensified in 1947, when pilot Kenneth Arnold was flying his plane over the Cascade Mountains in the USA. While searching for a missing aircraft he noticed nine strange lights in the sky. He later told newspaper reporters that they moved 'like a saucer when

Are UFOs visiting the West Pennine Moors?

you throw it along the top of water', and from this statement the term 'flying saucer' evolved.

The more technical term Unidentified Flying Object (UFO) was later created. This has come to mean that something moving in the sky which cannot immediately be explained, has been reported. Later it may be 'identified', or indeed found to be not an 'object' at all, but merely a light.

One of the most famous reported sightings in Lancashire came on the 15 February 1954, from two boys who were walking over Coniston Old Man, which before boundary changes was the highest mountain in the county. Suddenly they came upon a strange object which was hovering in the air above the fellside. Being a keen photographer, one of the boys had his camera with him and was able to take several photos. Although out of focus, the outline of the UFO was found to be similar to others which had been taken in the USA, so the event was given worldwide press coverage.

In the fifties flying saucer reports had become more frequent, but many sceptics did not yet take them seriously. One lighter moment came from the House of Commons when the MP for Heywood and Royton asked the Air Minister whether he knew about 'the thing' which had alarmed some of his constituents. He was told that 'this object did not emanate from outer space but from a laundry in Rochdale!'

Laughter followed as it was explained that a laundry mechanic from Wardle village, near Rochdale, had decided to find out the path of local air currents. He sent up five small hydrogen-filled balloons which were illuminated by flashlight bulbs. These had been seen by villagers who, in the dark, thought they were UFOs.

The sixties brought a spate of more serious UFO sightings in England which took many forms, ranging from pulsating lights to flying crosses. Many of these UFO reports came from policemen, perhaps because they are often out of doors during the night when UFOs are most likely to be seen and also they are trained to be observant. One of these came in May 1966 from St Helens, reported by a policeman who was at home on sick leave. Gazing out of the window on a dull day, both he and his wife saw six UFOs travelling in a south-easterly direction. They appeared to be 'white and glowing', one was large with a cup-shaped dome, and the other smaller ones were oval.

The following year a remarkable report came from a Bacup policeman. It began when he experienced crackling on the radio inside the police station. He went outside to check the aerial, but was amazed to see a cigar-shaped UFO hovering overhead. This UFO report, later verified by two other policemen, was different from many others in that it was not simply a distant light but more what many would regard as a spacecraft. It appeared to be metallic with portholes along its side, but with no obvious means of propulsion. He estimated it to be about ten feet in diameter and fifty feet long and it gave off a bright glow. It made a whirring sound as it hovered for several minutes about 80 metres (250ft) above the ground, then rose vertically upwards, disappearing into the sky.

In 1984 there came a large number of mysterious sightings from the hill country between Bacup and Todmorden which caught the attention of the national press, who named it the 'Valley of the UFOs'. Two girls who had been riding near Bacup were leading their ponies back to the stable when they saw a bright light in the sky. Suddenly it came zooming low down until it was only about 10 metres (30ft) above them. They could now see other lights of blue, red and green. Their frightened horses bolted towards the stable, followed by the girls, who, as they ran, seemed to be chased by the lights.

A local fishmonger told how he was driving on a moorland road near the town when a bright light suddenly appeared in front of him. He stopped his van, then watched in amazement as the light shot vertically upwards into the sky. Another man from Todmorden who was looking out of the window of his home saw a piercing bright white light hovering over Eagle Crag, lighting up the sky. He then saw a blue light and the outline of an object which he said was shaped like a helmet.

Two brothers, puzzled by all the alleged UFO sightings around Bacup, decided one night to go into the hills to investigate. Suddenly they were astounded to see a big light appear in the sky. The light, which came from a circular craft which gave out a high-pitched hum, began to fall rapidly towards them, then it hovered at about 300 feet in silence. Beneath it they saw triangular pads and orange-coloured lights.

Another report came from a policeman in Salford CID who was returning home early one morning. As he drove to Heywood, he saw a brilliant white circular object in the sky, moving towards the Rossendale Valley. Suddenly it stopped, then, after turning through 90 degrees, it sped off at an enormous speed towards the horizon. He was convinced that no aircraft could ever have attained such a speed.

There have also been hundreds of UFO reports from the West Pennine Moors, to the north of Bolton, stretching back to the fifties. In 1954 a couple at Farnworth saw a flying saucer speeding through the sky at Holcombe Brook, and three years later a yellow ball of fire was seen above Rivington. In 1969 a woman and her young daughter saw a mysterious object hovering over the rooftops of Bolton, then three days later a UFO was seen to land on a golf course at Farnworth.

Anglezarke Moor, Belmont and Rivington Pike seem to attract UFOs, for unexplained lights and strange craft moving through the sky above the hilltops are frequently reported. At an isolated farm at nearby Edgworth a family claimed to have been terrified by a UFO in 1985. The shapeless white glow, which stayed near their home for three hours, seemed to menacingly increase in size as the family watched. Its presence horrified the occupants, but Air Traffic Control at Manchester could not locate it on their radar.

In 1996 a report was made public which was said by sky-watchers to be 'a milestone in official recognition of the phenomenon of UFOs', for it came from two respected British Airways pilots. Flight 5061 from Milan had been approaching Manchester Airport on the 6 January 1995 when a near miss occurred. A strange craft, 'illuminated by white lights like a Christmas tree', came very close then hurled past them. The investigation that followed failed to find a convincing explanation, but ufologists believe it was another encounter with the Silent Vulcan. This is a mysterious craft, similar in shape to the old Vulcan Bomber, which has been sighted for over twenty years. It seems to frequent the Pennine Corridor, which stretches from the Midlands through Lancashire to the Scottish Border.

Have Aliens Landed?

Many of the UFO incidents which are reported in our newspapers are found after investigation to have rational explanations. This is particularly true of fast-moving lights which can result from a host of sources including conventional aircraft, satellites, meteorites or reflections from high-powered searchlights or laser shows. It has also been suggested that others, not so easily explained away, may be rare natural phenomena such as ball lightening or plasma. However, some people claim to have had close encounters which defy these explanations. They have seen features on UFOs, such as portholes and exhaust trails which suggest they are, in fact, types of aircraft or spacecraft.

A security guard who was working on a hospital building site in Burnley in 1986 saw a UFO which convinced him it was a type of spacecraft. It appeared during daylight, was saucer-shaped, of a grey metallic colour and 'as big as a bungalow'. It hovered very low at about tree-top height for several minutes. 'I could have hit it with a stone,' he later recalled. He was able to see what appeared to be flames shooting out from twin exhausts which curved downwards from some kind of engine, before it shot silently away at a very high speed. He speculated that it might have been a secret military aircraft, but why this would be tested over a highly populated area in daylight remains a mystery.

There are, of course, many people who believe that UFOs are sophisticated spacecraft which have been built and are piloted by aliens who are visiting earth. These 'beings' have been the subject of science-fiction literature and films for decades, which tends to undermine any serious theories regarding their existence. However, there are hundreds of well-documented reports from all over the world, including Lancashire, which tell of alien contact, and in some cases abduction by aliens. Others turn to folklore to point out that this is nothing new, for tales of goblins, elves and children taken by fairies are really tales of alien encounters thousands of years ago.

The most controversial alien incident of recent times happened in Rosswell, New Mexico, USA, in 1947, when following a raging storm a rancher reported that something had crashed on his land. It was officially stated that the wreckage was of a weather balloon, but it has since been claimed by many witnesses that this was a cover-up as a UFO had crashed and six aliens had been found, one still alive.

But at least one alien encounter in Lancashire pre-dates the Rosswell incident. In November 1926 a young Bolton boy believed he saw three adult-sized aliens in silver-grey suits. However, it was during the spate of UFO sightings that occurred in 1984 around the Rossendale Valley, that several intriguing reports of aliens made press headlines. One man at Crawshawbooth was closing his garage door after returning home from work when he saw two figures from the corner of his eye. Turning around he was astonished to see that they were clothed in brilliantly polished silver suits. Their heads were enclosed in helmets and their faces featureless, and they were carrying what looked like a metal bar. The rustle of their clothing was heard, but as the man looked away for a brief second they vanished.

Four miles away at Newchurch, two teenage boys were out shooting in the local woods when they saw a bright unexplained light in the sky, glimmering through the trees. In fright they began to run, but then found their path blocked by a tall figure who was covered from head to foot in a shining black cloak. He appeared to have a large forehead and did not move, so after a few seconds the boys turned around and ran quickly away.

In 1996 a man and his wife began to experience a series of unexplained happenings in their home in Horwich. These including odd noises and objects being mysteriously moved or appearing from nowhere. Each of them believed at first that the other was playing a joke, but later when they realised this was not the case they became alarmed. Their problems became even worse when the husband began sleep walking during the night. This led him to contact a paranormal investigator who regressed him to try to find the cause of the trouble. Under a hypnotic trance he was astonished to see small, grey alien creatures with wide eyes and slit-mouths. This has led him to believe that at some point in his life he has been abducted by aliens and that they are responsible for the turmoil within his house. He has also developed a strange blister on his leg which skin specialists have so far been unable to fully explain.

Chapter Three

Ghostly Encounters

The Supernatural

The widespread belief in the existence of ghosts which is apparent today forges a link to prehistoric times as many of our primitive ancestors believed that death was not the end, but that the human spirit moved on to another world. However, this spirit or soul of man often wished to remain on earth, and if it did so, great misfortune could result. It was, consequently, in the interests of those who remained to ensure that the spirits were given every help in their journey to the next world. This may well explain the huge Bronze Age burial mounds which are to be found in many parts of Lancashire. These constructions, with the simple resources of the day, are an incredible achievement. No doubt elaborate funeral rites would have been carried out at these sites to appease the unseen spirits, and the striking presence of the mounds would stand as a reminder of the necessity of Ancestor Worship.

But in spite of these precautions, on occasions the spirits became earthbound, causing terror to all around. Some took up permanent residence in rivers and wells, others on high hilltops or deep in rocky caves – places which still remain part of haunted Lancashire.

Even the coming of Christianity, which brought with it a more complicated but less fearful view of the next world, has been unable to change this deep-rooted belief in ghosts. Although many people leave the great mystery of life and death to a simple faith, others speculate on what remains largely unexplained. And those who have actually seen or felt the presence of a ghost cannot fail to acknowledge the evidence that has appeared before their own eyes.

It is said that more women than men believe in ghosts, and that certain individuals are 'psychic', which allows them to frequently see or even attract spirits. But for a sceptic to be told by a psychic that a ghost is present but invisible is hardly convincing evidence. So although the shelves of the Society of Psychical Research are bulging with records of hauntings, the debate still continues. Science plays a minor role in proving the presence of ghosts as most hauntings are spontaneous. Although unexplained changes in temperature, strange noises and vague shapes have been recorded in haunted houses by ghost hunters, this is seldom completely convincing to outsiders.

It is more often the personal testimony of individuals who have had chance encounters with ghosts that provides the greatest challenge to the unbeliever. Those who might have a commercial interest in having a ghost on their premises, such as owners of stately homes, are immediately dismissed as being suspect. Those of integrity who remain, particularly if more that one person has witnessed the haunting at the same time, are the strongest proof that ghosts do exist.

In Lancashire ghosts have been seen in many forms. These hauntings may begin in a simple way such as a sudden feeling of coldness in a room, the overwhelming smell of perfume or tobacco, or the unexplained sound of laughter or footsteps in empty houses. More striking is the materialisation of human images which may start as vague, misty shapes, then become partial or even complete forms. Often dressed in the fashion of their day, these ghosts seem to be unaware of or even uninterested in those who see them, offering no threat but being intent on carrying out some perceived ritual. The exception is the poltergeist which can be frightening to the onlooker, as in a bout of frenzied emotion it has been known to throw items around a home and even cause fires.

So whether dismissed by the sceptic as imaginative rubbish, or upheld by the psychic as proven fact, ghosts are unlikely to ever go away. Seldom a week passes without a new haunting being recorded in our local newspapers, giving substance to the boast that Lancashire is England's most haunted county.

Pubs with Spirits

Over the centuries, Lancashire's old inns, as well as being a welcome refuge for weary travellers, have played their part in many of our historical intrigues. They began as simple refreshment places on our Roman roads, and were known as "tabernae diversorae", from which our term "tavern" has evolved. Both ale and mead had become popular drinks in Anglo-Saxon England, leading to the establishment of ale-houses, then inns which began to offer accommodation. Fortunately, many of the ancient Lancashire hostelries have survived, their walls having witnessed so many fascinating events: undercover priests living the lives of secret agents, Royalist and Cromwellian soldiers planning their next battles, highwaymen and murderers evading the law, and eloping lovers hiding from irate fathers. So it is not surprising, given such a rich tapestry of human activity, that many are said to be haunted.

Limbrick is a hamlet which nestles on the edge of the West Pennine Moors close to Chorley. On Long Lane stands the Black Horse Hotel, a pub which in 1997 celebrated an amazing 'thousand years of pulling pints'. According to tradition, it was sixty nine years before the Norman Conquest when the doors were first opened, then in 1577 it became the second pub in England to be given a licence. This marvellous hostelry echoes with memories of the past, locals often talking of mysterious happenings they have experienced within the building. Unexplained ghostly noises are heard, with ice-cold unseen hands falling on unsuspecting shoulders, creating a mysterious atmosphere which American ghost hunters cannot resist.

Rich in folklore, Rossendale's windswept moorland valleys hide many ghostly hostelries. At Waterfoot the Railway Inn is said to be haunted by Jane, a grey lady who glides through the walls. Unexplained noises occur at dead of night, items mysteriously disappear and the cellar suddenly becomes unusually cold. Owd Betts, a pub popular with walkers who climb nearby Whittle Hill, has the ghost of its former landlady, while the Duckworth Hall Inn at Oswaldtwistle is haunted by a Victorian man.

It is not surprising that Liverpool, a unique city with a colourful history, has many haunted pubs. It is believed that a former landlord of the Coach and Horses in Everton, who hanged himself, now haunts the building. Known affectionately as George, the spirit sometimes appears transparent and at other times completely solid. Both the Poste House in Cumberland Street and The Castle in Everton have spectral old women, while The Philharmonic in Hope Street has a ghostly old man who brings luck to gamblers.

Affetside is an isolated village which stands high on a ridge on the line of a former Roman road, north-west of Bury. At its centre stands the ancient Pack Horse Inn, a building that dates back to 1443. Visitors are often startled when they order their first pint, for staring out at them from above the bar is a mahogany-coloured human skull. It is said to be that of George Whewell, a local man who executed James, seventh Earl of Derby, at Bolton in 1651. But beware if the skull has been disturbed, for the pub becomes filled with supernatural activity.

At Foulridge, near Colne, it is the New Inn that has gained a widespread reputation for being haunted. Some say the ghosts of Quakers glide through the pub, angry because their tombstones from the local burial ground have been disturbed. Others believe that the apparition is of a Cavalier killed by his Cromwellian enemies at nearby Hobstones Farm. Legends of the supernatural abound in the area, with tales of ghostly Civil War soldiers being seen riding across the meadows.

The George Hotel in Church Street, Preston, is a fine building that served as a coaching inn during the 18th century. When builders broke an old grave slab which lined the cellar floor and discovered a white bereavement ring with the name Robert Clay engraved upon it, supernatural forces began to take over. The landlord and his family began to be disturbed by unexplained noises during the night. Then the ghost of a Victorian man was seen on the stairs, followed by the chilling re-enactment of a woman in 17th-century dress stabbing a man. Mediums who were called in told the landlord that the pub lay on an ancient burial ground and that Robert Clay, the man named on the ring, was himself a murderer. After abusing two girls he had killed them, burying their bodies in a hidden cellar beneath the pub's present cellar!

Delightful Chipping is one of the gems of the Ribble Valley, a village noted for its cheese-making and chair factory. The Sun Inn hides a sad tale of unrequited love. It is haunted by the ghost of Lizzy Dean, a serving wench who worked at the inn in 1835, and who was engaged to be married to a local man. However, her wedding day quickly turned from joy to sorrow as she gazed out of the window of the pub and saw her bridegroom walking from the church with his new bride, whom he had married instead of Lizzy. Devastated by the event, the twenty-year-old hanged herself in the pub, where her spirit still walks. In a final bid for retribution, she requested that her body be buried on the church pathway. Her ex-fiancee would them have to walk over her resting place each Sunday, reminding him of his terrible deed.

The Radcliffe Arms in Oldham was once haunted by the ghost of a man who hanged himself in the cellar many years ago, while the Rake Inn near Rochdale has a more jolly faced Cavalier apparition. At rural Mawdesley, near Chorley, the Black Bull had a reputation last century for attracting the rowdy element. Every Sunday morning the landlord would go around the pub gathering up ears and noses which had been severed in the Saturday night fights! The revellers would occasionally be joined by the local ghost from Mawdesley Old Hall who did not wish to be left out of the fun. The landlord managed to capture the spirit in a bottle, which he placed on display before finally tossing it in a local pit.

The ancient Ring 'O' Bells pub in Middleton, near Manchester, is reputed to be haunted by the ghost of Lord Stannycliffe's son who was murdered during the Civil War. He was a staunch Royalist who happened to be in the inn when a band of Roundheads entered the building. Outnumbered, he decided to hide in the cellar, hoping his enemies would soon depart. Unfortunately, they continued to drink for some time, making the landlord more and more agitated, fearing that if the hidden Royalist was discovered he, too, would pay the price. Eventually the landlord could stand the suspense no longer, so he told the Roundheads where the young aristocrat lay hidden. A valiant attempt was made to escape by following a secret tunnel which led to the church. Sadly, he was unsuccessful, being overtaken by the Roundheads in the churchyard and savagely murdered. It is said that his remains still lie beneath a stone slab in the cellar and many people have reported seeing his ghost, clothed in the Cavalier fashion of the period.

House of Terror

In 1993 a terrifying incident occurred in Westhoughton which led a local historian to claim that it is the most haunted town in Britain. The horror began in an innocent way at a semi-detached council house in Wingates Grove, at 7.30 one Saturday evening. In one of the children's bedrooms, their 32-year-old father noticed that small drops of water had started to form. Suspecting a water leak from the plumbing system, he went into the loft to check but found it was perfectly dry. However, the water on the ceiling appeared to be getting worse so the next day a workman was called in to investigate, but he too was unable to detect any leak.

The problem persisted, with the water now appearing in all the rooms in the house except the bathroom. Again the council workmen were called in, and again they were completely baffled. They removed the floor boards to find it completely dry underneath, yet the ceilings were becoming saturated with water.

Early on the following Monday afternoon, the young son told his father that a picture had fallen off its hanger on the wall downstairs. The man went to investigate, but as he arrived in the room, with a number of council officials looking on, a porcelain horse suddenly left the mantelpiece and zoomed across the room. Another council official then confessed that she had also seen crockery and cutlery acting in the same way. There was obviously something very strange happening in the property.

Both perplexed and horrified by the spirits which the family now believed were creating havoc in their house, they then sought the help of the local vicar. He came immediately to their home where he began to offer up prayers. Unfortunately, this did not work for after he had left objects again began to fly around the rooms. By this time the whole family had become distraught so the local council arranged alternative accommodation for them in a flat.

It then became apparent that the upheaval only occurred when the young son was in the vicinity. When he was sent to a neighbour's home the spirit seemed to follow him, with ornaments being thrown about. The ordeal continued in their temporary flat when for no apparent reason a fire started among some clothes and other objects flew across the room.

To try to solve the problem a medium from Atherton, who was an expert on the paranormal, was called in to investigate. He carried out an exorcism in the house, then spoke of his conclusions. After talking with the boy he found that he had been playing with a Ouija board while at school and learned that other people living near the house had also dabbled with the board. This, he believed, had created an open access to the spirit world. Three spirits had been identified as causing the disturbance, one was in the house and the other two within the boy himself. The exorcism cleared away these unwanted intruders from the spirit world, but he warned of the terrible dangers that can lie in amusing oneself with the occult, which for this Westhoughton family was certainly no joke.

Over the years there have been many claims of mysterious happenings at different sites within the town. The Ex-Servicemen's Club is said to be haunted by a 'woman in red' and ghostly footsteps and unexplained noises have been heard at the Central Labour Club. On one occasion a foreign student who was visiting the town told how he had seen a complete re-enactment of a Civil War battle which had taken place at Hoghton Common.

In 1996 the landlord of the Wheatchief told how his pub had also been invaded by a ghost. This strange apparition, which has been seen by many customers, leaves an odd shadow which suddenly vanishes. On one terrifying occasion the landlord's girlfriend attempted to talk to the ghost, which then seemed to take over her voice, but the words she spoke could not be understood. A medium who has investigated the hauntings believes it is not one, but four spirits which are responsible.

A woman who lived for over twenty years in a house in Tempest Road at nearby Chew Moor, spoke in 1989 of the ghost her family had come to accept. The apparition was that of a lady in a long, flowing robe who had been seen at different times by each member of the household. After the first initial shock they became unconcerned about the presence, but it was not accepted by the family dog. He would growl at the ghost, his hair would stand on end, then sensibly he would dash from the room!

So why does Westhoughton seem to have so many ghosts? Some people believe that the terrible Prestoria Pit Disaster, which occurred locally in 1910 killing 344 men, may somehow be responsible.

Paslew's Ghost

The tranquil ruins of Whalley Abbey stand close to the banks of the Calder in this popular corner of the Ribble Valley. For 250 years the chanting of the Cistercian monks echoed through the cloisters, but they were silenced in 1537 – Henry VIII, ever striving for more power and wealth, had been determined to make the estate his own.

But Abbot John Paslew was equally determined that he would not give up this house of God without a fight. He was a striking figure who had been born in the nearby village of Wiswell, then taken a degree in divinity at Oxford. For thirty years he had been in charge of the Abbey, giving both religious guidance to the monks and administering the many possessions which the abbey had throughout Lancashire. The annual income from this land would be at least £60 000 at today's value, which had not gone unnoticed by the King.

Although John Paslew was not directly involved in the violence of the rebellion known as the Pilgrimage of Grace, his conscience would not allow him to take the Oath of Allegiance. So, following a trial held at Lancaster on the 9th March 1537, he was executed the next day close to the castle, having been found guilty of high treason. His death was said to have been foretold by a former monk of Whalley named Edmund Howard whose ghost had appeared before the Abbot in 1520 telling him 'he would live sixteen years and no more'. However, a local tradition conflicts with the records of his death, for it says that he was hung at the monastery gates and buried in Whalley churchyard. A gravestone within the church is believed by some to have been from his tomb.

Abbot Paslew's ghost is said to haunt Whalley Abbey

But it seems that John Paslew does not rest easy in his grave, wherever that may be, for his ghost has been seen for centuries around Whalley. In 1966 there were a series of sightings, a girl saw his shadowy presence in Pendle Road and a press photographer was even able to catch him on film. Chanting has been heard drifting from the empty ruins, ghostly footsteps are frequently heard in the conference centre which has been built in the grounds, and two astonished students even saw a procession of phantom monks.

After John Paslew had died for his faith, all the property which had belonged to the abbey was forfeited. In 1553 the manor of Whalley was bought by John Braddyll of Brockhall and Richard Assheton of Lever, Bolton. But with this property came a curse on all members of the Assheton family, who since 1558 have lived at Downham. It is said that if any of them steps upon the grave of Abbot Paslew they will die within a year.

Animal Apparitions

Although many Christians believe that, unlike humans, animals do not possess souls, there are numerous examples of animal ghosts being seen throughout Lancashire. The black dog, commemorated on so many northern inn signs, is perhaps the most commonly seen apparition. Known locally as Gytrash, Striker or Padfoot, its piercing call is said to be an omen of death. It was also the familiar of witches, being their link with the Devil and the source of many menacing occult activities.

Just a few years ago I was told about a young soldier who met the ghostly animal at Bradshaw near Bolton. He was home on leave from his posting in Germany and walking at dusk along a pathway near the village when he saw a black dog approaching him. Being fond of animals, he bent down ready to pat it. Suddenly it leapt into the air then, before his eyes, it simply melted away. Although at the peak of physical fitness through his army training, he was greatly shocked by the event. He returned home pale and upset, and it was many months before he could talk openly about what he had seen.

At Cliviger near Burnley a pack of the ghostly black hounds are said to bound from the moors on Hallowe'en, while another pack appeared regularly at Droysden. At Little Hulton and Clitheroe there are ancient wells that are said to be haunted by the animals, while Preston and Manchester have headless strikers.

At Blackburn it is not ghostly black dogs, but phantom horses which reputedly haunt the town. Recently a local woman told me how her mother had been waiting in a queue at a bus stop in the Mill Hill area. Suddenly she was astonished to see a large herd of snorting horses come galloping down the road. She gasped at the strange site, then turned towards the other people in the queue to find out their reactions. She was even more astonished to find that they were quite unmoved, for they had seen nothing unusual. Only later did she learn that the phantom horses had been seen in previous years in the same spot and also in the fields near Tockholes village. And on mist-shrouded Noon Hill, which lies about seven miles away on the edge of Rivington Moor, a ghostly horseman is said to lure travellers to their deaths in the boggy peat.

Perhaps the most famous of Lancashire's animal apparitions is the spectral horseman of Wycoller, which for centuries has been haunting this lovely moorland village. It is associated with the romantic ruins of Wycoller Hall, which stand open to the sky, reached by a twin-arched bridge which spans a fast-moving beck. It was once the home of the Cunliffe family, then last century it was immortalised by Charlotte Brontë as Ferndean Manor in *Jane Eyre*.

It is said locally that each year, during the height of winter, the spectral horseman gallops down the valley towards the hall. He then quickly dismounts, dashes through the door and up the stairs. The horrific screams of a woman echo from the building, followed by an intense sobbing, then a poignant silence. The ghostly figure returns to his horse, which he remounts, then speeds off into the eerie darkness. It is believed to be a re-enactment of a murder which took place at the hall during the 17th century, when a Cunliffe killed his wife, but not before she correctly prophesied the downfall of the family.

But at the hamlet of Crank, near St Helens, it is a ghostly white rabbit which is still feared by local people as a sign of misfortune. Its origins can be traced to the early 17th century, when an old, foreign woman lived with her six-year-old granddaughter named Jenny and her pet white rabbit, in a cottage at the foot of a hill. The old woman, who was said by some to be a witch, had a quarrel with her rich but morose neighbour, a farmer named Pullen. He had asked her to try to clear him of a wasting disease by using herbal medicine, but had come to the conclusion that instead, she had tried to poison him. Feeling bewitched, he knew that traditionally her spell could only be broken if he drew blood from her body. So with this in mind, he enlisted the help of a local thug named Dick Piers.

One night the two men broke into the old lady's cottage, but the noise woke Jenny who saw them cutting the arm of her grandmother. Frightened by the sight, she grabbed her devoted rabbit then dashed from the building towards the chapel. She managed to escape from Piers who had chased after her, but then in a bout of frustration he brutally kicked the animal to death. Sadly, the dead body of Jenny was also found the next day; she had fallen exhausted against the chapel wall and died from her injuries.

However, this was not to be the end of the affair, for a month later Piers was terrified to see the ghost of Jenny's white rabbit following him towards the village. Shocked by the sight of the animal which he knew he had killed, his body was later discovered in a quarry on Billinge Hill: he had committed suicide. Pullen, at first unmoved by the sinister events, was himself to become the second victim of the ghostly animal. It pursued him across the fields where he died from fright and exhaustion.

Haunted Halls

Many members of Lancashire's ancient families have grown up since childhood accepting the presence of ghosts, for virtually every old hall in the county seems to have a resident apparition. White ladies, grey-cowled monks, spectral horses and wispy, shadowy figures are just a few of the many different ghostly manifestations which glide through these old homes. Their fabric, having witnessed upwards of five hundred years of turbulent history, seems to have absorbed some of the intrigues and emotions of past events. Then quite suddenly, in dramatic fashion, this is released in the form of a spirit which seems bound to re-enact one of these traumatic episodes.

The half-timbered splendour of Speke Hall lies close to the banks of the River Mersey, seven miles from the centre of Liverpool. Reached over a sandstone bridge which spans a dried-up moat, the present building dates from the 15th century and is the ancestral home of the Norris family. Here during penal times, Roman Catholic priests were landed from the river under cover of darkness, then hidden before beginning their missionary work.

It is the Tapestry Room at Speke that is reputed to be haunted by the ghost of Mary Norris, the last heiress of the family. In 1731 she married Lord Sidney Beauclerk who was the grandson of King Charles II and his mistress Nell Gwynn. He turned out to be a repulsive character who began to gamble away his wife's fortune. Distressed into madness by his outrageous behaviour and weakened by the birth of her first child, Mary took the baby to a window where she threw it down into the moat below. She then dashed down into the Great Hall where she ended her own life. Her spirit is said to wander through the Tapestry Room, where unseen hands gently rock a cradle backwards and forwards.

At medieval Rufford Old Hall near Ormskirk, there have been many sitings over the years of a grey lady who is believed to be Elizabeth Hesketh, a daughter of this ancient Lancashire family. In the late 16th century she was betrothed to a handsome suitor who went off to fight in the Dutch wars. He died in battle, an event which shocked Elizabeth, and from which she never recovered. Her apparition, draped in Elizabethan dress, still wanders through the building awaiting the lover who never returned. On one occasion she suddenly appeared before a curator at the hall who was playing the piano; he thought that perhaps she had been attracted by the music.

Samlesbury Hall, which lies between Preston and Blackburn, is a magnificent manor house that has seen many amazing changes over the centuries. It was built in 1325 by Gilbert de Southworth as a home for his new bride, Alice D'Ewyas. It remained the residence of the Southworth family for over 300 years, then in 1678 it was sold to Thomas Braddyll. The Braddyll

Lovely Samlesbury Hall has a ghostly White Lady

family never lived at the hall, but rented it out to seven local families who were hand-loom weavers.

In 1830, following the decline in hand-loom weaving, the hall was put to another use when it opened as a beer-house. It was frequented by navvies who were building the new Preston to Blackburn turnpike road. This ended in 1850 when it was bought by John Cooper, who rented it out to a Yorkshire woman for use as a residential school for young girls. Twelve years later it was bought by a Blackburn iron-founder, Joseph Harrison, who entertained Charles Dickens at the hall in 1869. But following the Harrison's financial decline, it then became the residence of the Mayor of Blackburn, Fred Baynes, who lived in the hall until 1909. Then unoccupied, it fell into a dilapidated state, and by 1924 was on the point of being demolished. Thankfully, a successful appeal was launched to save the building, which under the guidance of a body of trustees has now survived and been restored to its former glory.

Not surprisingly, having seen so many changes, the hall is reputed to be haunted: the White Lady of Samlesbury being one of Lancashire's most famous ghosts. Over a long period, many people claim to have seen the wispy apparition drifting through the building. Only recently I was speaking to a Blackburn woman who told me that her mother, while attending a dance some years ago at the hall, definitely saw the white lady.

The ghost is believed to be that of Dorothy, a daughter of Sir John Southworth who lived during the 17th century. She is said to have fallen in love with the son of the nearby Hoghton family, but unfortunately, due to religious differences, her father would not give his consent to the marriage. The Southworths were staunch Roman Catholics who refused to give up their faith, while the Hoghtons had become Protestants.

Secretly she plotted to elope with her lover, but this plan was overheard by her brothers who then waited at the rendezvous point. A frenzied fight followed during which her lover was killed, his body being then buried near the hall. Sir John Southworth sent his disgraced daughter abroad to spend her life in a convent. She never forgot the pain of the terrible event, her mind breaking under the strain, and after her death her spirit returned to seek out the hidden grave of her lover.

As well as being seen inside the building, the white lady has been recorded both in the grounds and drifting along the road close to the hall. It is believed that the hidden grave of her lover was discovered some years ago when a human skeleton was uncovered in the grounds.

Dunkenhalgh Hall at Clayton-le-Moors near Accrington, now a popular hotel, was once the home of the Walmesley family, then the Petre family. The latter, during the early 18th century, employed a French governess named Lucette who is said to have fallen in love with a handsome visitor to the hall. When she became pregnant he refused to marry her, so in a fit of depression she drowned herself in the nearby River Hyndburn. Her white-shrouded ghost has been seen in the hotel grounds around Christmas time, drifting up to the old bridge from where she plunged nearly three centuries ago.

It is believed to be the ghost of Sir John Towneley whose heavy footsteps are heard in his ancestral home of Towneley Hall near Burnley. Now a fine museum, the dancing lights, echoing voices and unexplained noises which are sometimes experienced by both staff and visitors, are said to evolve from his tortured spirit for during his lifetime he caused great misery to many of his tenants by evicting them from their homes.

Heskin Hall near Chorley, which dates back to Elizabethan times, is also reputed to have periods when unexplained noises emit from the Scarlet Room. These are said to come from the drifting apparition of the White Maiden, which is the spirit of a young girl who was hanged during the Civil War. An icy coldness suddenly falls in parts of the haunted room and the stern-faced ghost of one of Cromwell's followers has also been seen.

Other Lancashire Halls which also have their resident spirits include popular Park Hall at Charnock Richard, which has a white lady who rises from a lake; Borwick Hall near Lancaster which has the ghost of a girl who was starved to death; Turton Tower at Bolton, home of the Timberbottom Skulls, where a black lady glides up a staircase and a cradle, like that at Speke Hall, is rocked by invisible hands; and Worsley Old Hall, near Manchester, where the ghost of Dorothy Legh, robed in a green dress, tumbles down the stairs.

However, it is not only those halls which have survived the passing of time which are haunted, for several ruined halls still retain their ghosts. In the West Pennine Moors, close to the village of Tockholes, lies the isolated ruins of Hollinshead Hall, once the home of the Brock-Hollinshead family. Only the ancient Well House now survives, the water trickling from the head of a grotesque stone gargoyle, known as the Spewing Laddie.

A son of the last generation to live in the hall fell in love with a local village girl. His father decided the girl was unsuitable so to cool the boy's ardour he locked him in the Well House overnight. What terrible events unfolded before him during his brief captivity is not known, but the next morning he was completely deranged and remained so for many years. There have been many reports of ghosts seen in the ruins, including that of a cavalier who was seen praying for victory in a forthcoming battle.

Spooky Bolton

With its impressive Victorian Town Hall and array of up-market shops, modern Bolton has acquired a glittering image which attracts many visitors throughout the year. Few of the people who come to the town to buy gifts or visit the Octagon Theatre, however, are aware of its secret face – Bolton has many haunted sites with the theatre itself having a resident ghost!

Bolton: one of Lancashire's most haunted towns

Bradshawgate, which lies in the town centre, is a lively street full of hotels, shops, restaurants and attractive pubs, but on a dark November evening in 1940 an event took place there that was to cast a shadow over the area. The body of Minnie Stott, a 17-year-old shop worker who lived in Clarendon Street in the town, was found that night down a narrow alleyway. She had been brutally strangled, it is said by a soldier who was wearing mufti, but her killer was never identified or brought to justice.

Many believe that the spirit of Minnie still haunts the site of her murder, perhaps never being able to rest in peace while the crime remains unsolved. There have been many sightings of her ghost, one of the most dramatic occurred in 1987. This was witnessed by a young girl who perhaps unknowingly had an affinity to the murder victim for at the time she, too, was 17 years old.

She worked as a cleaner at the car showrooms of Parker's garage on Bradshawgate, which lies adjacent to the scene of the crime. At the top of a flight of stairs she suddenly saw a misty apparition form which was unmistakably that of a young girl. The eerie sight terrified her. 'I have never felt so frightened in my life,' she said later. Up till the time she saw the ghost she had been completely unaware of Minnie's murder or the reputation that the site had for being haunted. However, another worker related how she, too, had noticed that the temperature of the building would suddenly drop for no apparent reason.

Just off Bradshawgate is Wood Street, a cobbled backwater of attractive Georgian houses. On the wall of one of these a plaque proudly states that 'William Hesketh Lever was born here on the 19th September 1851'. This building, once the home of the founder of a great soap empire and now Bolton Socialist Club, has also gained a reputation for being haunted.

In 1972 the ghostly forms of a man and a woman wearing Victorian-style clothes were seen in the building. Then eight years later the club president told how he had felt his shoulder being touched by an invisible hand. Another sighting followed in 1987 when a former local councillor went along to the club one Sunday morning to do some work. Although completely alone in the building, he sensed a strange, party atmosphere. He was then amazed to see a man, dressed in a Victorian-style hat and long coat glide down the stairs in front of him. The man then completely disappeared near a locked door.

Around the corner in Churchgate stands the town's oldest building, the half-timbered Old Man and Scythe pub, whose history goes back to 1251. It was here in 1651 that the ill-fated 7th Earl of Derby spent his last hour on earth before being executed just outside. So it is not surprising that the pub has witnessed several mysterious happenings.

In 1996 the licensee told how a woman customer who rose from her chair was appalled to find that her hand, although uninjured, was dripping with blood. The blood ran profusely from her hand onto the floor. Shocked by the incident, she quickly left the building with her two friends. The barman, who thought the blood had dripped through the ceiling onto the woman's hand, dashed upstairs to see if someone had been injured but he could find no reason for the incident.

A psychic is said to have detected a ghostly presence along the pub hallway and there have been many other mysterious happenings in the building. A service engineer was in the cellar when he heard a voice call out to him but there was no one there. The ghost of a woman is said to move around upstairs, and some years ago a man was seen at the bar talking to another ghost!

Just across the road from the pub is the site of the former Capital Cinema, which was demolished in 1988. Even in its heyday, when it was one of the most popular venues in the town, there were many reports of strange, unexplained happenings in the building. One came from a young projectionist who later hanged himself in a storeroom. The building was then converted for use as a bingo hall and sports club, but still odd noises and reports of ghosts continued.

When the site was flattened and the old cinema replaced by a modern office block it was anticipated that it would be the end of the spooky goings-on, but this has proved not to be the case. For staff in what is now a tax office tell of eerie noises, typewriters and lights being mysteriously being turned on, and doors being opened and closed when no one is in the room. Night cleaners have also reported seeing the ghostly presence of a woman in their fourth floor rest room.

Theatre lovers who flock in to enjoy the latest performance at Bolton's renowned Octagon Theatre are usually blissfully unaware of what is happening behind the scenes. But one activity they most certainly do not know about is the presence of the Theatre ghost. It is believed to be that of Fida, the Octagon's first wardrobe mistress, who died while working at the theatre. The ghost has been seen gliding across the gallery and in the control box, it has also been blamed for suddenly turning lights on and even working the sewing machines in the wardrobe room.

But in spite of Bolton's ghostly reputation for mysterious happenings, one couple were happy to return to the town because of a Yorkshire ghost. They had been the landlords at the Duck and Firkin pub in Bradshawgate before they moved to the ancient Golden Lion pub at Todmorden in 1986. During their six week residence in the building they were terrified by the sound of ghostly footsteps and strange murmuring during the night. It was said to be the restless spirit of Esmerelda, a woman who had been murdered in the building two hundred years ago. She had been strangled in what was now the ladies toilet, where visitors are still too afraid to venture alone.

Countryside Phantoms

Weeton is an ancient village which rests in rural seclusion on the Fylde, less than five miles from Blackpool. Once part of the Earl of Derby's estate, it is said that Oliver Cromwell stayed at the local Eagle and Child inn. The village can also boast a local martyr for Blessed William Harcourt was born here in 1609, then died for his faith at Tyburn in 1679. So in view of these rich historical connections it is hardly surprising that the village is reputed to be haunted. The main culprit is a hairy boggart or poltergeist which for centuries has been reported in the area. Nearby Manor Farm also has a cloaked apparition, while few locals will venture alone up Greenhalgh Lane at midnight for fear of seeing a ghostly coffin floating through the air.

Just six miles from Weeton lies Catforth, where the Roman Catholic church of St Robert contains a host of fascinating relics, including the severed head of a martyred priest. Here at Swillbrook House, which was formerly a school, the ghost of a child is said to roam. While at Gubberford Bridge, near Scorton, the grey apparition of a servant girl is sometimes seen staring into the water. She is said to have worked at Woodacre Hall, then been murdered by her jealous lover.

At Banks near Southport the tragic ghost of a woman is sometimes heard calling out the name of her husband Ralph, across the marshy Ribble estuary. He was a fisherman who perished in a storm in the treacherous Irish Sea. A few miles inland at Croston village about twenty years ago, the ghost of a small girl in a red shawl was seen by a school teacher. It is believed to have been that of Mary Ellen Hudson, whose sad epitaph written in 1890 was that she died 'friendless'.

Rivington, one of the most attractive corners of the West Pennine Moors, as well as possessing marvellous countryside has a host of ghosts. In 1967, on a clear bright morning, two workmen reported seeing a ghostly ultra-white shape gliding around Rivington Castle ruins. They watched in amazement as the shape moved backwards and forwards around the castle grounds before disappearing in a clump of bushes. "I've never seen anything so deeply white before," one of the men said later.

A cottage which lies half-hidden in trees close to popular Great House Barn at Rivington has had many strange happenings. These have been linked to a young boy who was tragically burned to death in the house. Sounds said to be like a table-tennis ball being batted backwards and forwards, footsteps in empty rooms and one visitor feeling an invisible cat on her bedclothes during the night have all been reported.

Some years ago, before the cottage had been renovated, in one bedroom the electric light would never work. Then one evening a visitor who was stopping at the house noticed that a light was pouring out from beneath the bedroom door. She went with the owner into the room where they found that the light bulb was burning brightly. When the switch was moved the light went out, but it would not come on again. It was decided that this was merely due to faulty wiring, so the next day an electrician was brought in. After climbing into the loft to check the wiring he said, 'There is no way that that light-bulb could ever be lit up. It is not even connected to the electricity supply!"

Less than two miles away at Anderton, near to a small grass verge which contains an ancient signpost known as Headless Cross, there have been many sitings of a cloaked ghost. Traditionally this is said to be that of Father Bennett, a priest from Lady Chapel which now lies beneath the waters of Lower Rivington Reservoir. Following the Reformation the priest took the chapel treasures away along a hidden tunnel, intending to hide them for safety, but he was never seen again. It is believed that he was murdered by thieves, who then buried his body. Since then his restless spirit has remained earthbound, ever-searching for the sacred vessels.

The ghost of Father Bennett has been blamed for several unexplained car accidents which have happened along a nearby road when motorists have been distracted by a grey figure which then vanishes. Two miles away at Horwich it is council staff who have been disturbed by a phantom who haunts the Public Hall. The ghostly man, said to be 'portly, middle-aged with sideburns' is thought to be that of a former councillor from pre-war days. Another apparition seen in the town is that of a knight who speeds by on a white horse, bringing an omen of impending bad health or even death.

Chapter Four

A Pagan Landscape

Lost Gods

Lancashire is a county which abounds with mysterious tales of the supernatural. Many of these are a legacy from a half-forgotten past for since pre-historic times wave upon wave of different races have made their home in our corner of England, each one bringing with them their own strange gods. On windswept hilltops, across lonely moorlands, and in quiet villages memories of these ancient pagan beliefs remain. The horned devil is said to lurk in high places; Jenny Greenteeth hides beneath the waters of our ponds and rivers; the terrifying green man lives in our woodland glades; while the snarling black dog is a messenger of evil.

These legends that have endured through so many centuries are a link to the dawn of the human race. Evidence of the first Lancastrians dates from around 12 000BC, when they were living in a region that we would find unrecognisable. At this time what we now know as the Irish Sea was largely a marshy land that stretched many miles westwards, linked to high points which are now the Isle of Man and Anglesey. The sea which now separates Lancashire from Ireland was just a fraction of its present width. Inland, where our familiar cities, towns and high moorlands now lie, was a vast forest full of wild cattle, boar and deer. It was the chance discovery of what has become known as the Poulton Elk, which dates from 10 000BC, that is an exciting link to this early period. Now housed in the Harris Museum at Preston, the animal was unearthed by a mechanical digger on the Fylde. What makes the find particularly significant is that before dying it had been wounded 17 times by stone weapons; man had arrived in Lancashire.

Flint tools and chippings found on several moorland sites and at such places as Ribchester and Walton-le-Dale show where these first Mesolithic Lancastrian families lived in camps during the next 6000 years. In appearance the men of these tribes are believed to have been robust, long-headed and with strongly-boned faces.

Intrinsic to these people was their belief in a supernatural power. Evidence in the form of carved statues found in many sites in Europe suggest that one of their earliest religions centred on the earth-mother, who was a Goddess of Fertility. These carved effigies of pregnant women, together with phallic symbols, sometimes discovered in shrines, show early man's fascination with creation. This concern with fertility is a theme which was to occur in many future beliefs, including the legacy of witchcraft which came into prominence in the 17th century.

About 3600BC other early settlers began to arrive in Lancashire from Europe. These Neolithic people, who were our first farmers, probably shared common religious beliefs in a fertility cult with the existing population, but were more skilled in the manufacture of tools and weapons. They also began the practice of constructing large earth mounds for their dead, around which revolved religious rites of which little is known.

A significant change came around 2000BC when what is believed to be the first of a series of Celtic immigrant tribes arrived in Britain for this marked the beginning of the Bronze Age. Known as the Beaker Folk from a distinctive design of pot which they produced, this energetic, nomadic race came from Spain, introducing the first metals to this country. A sherd of Beaker pottery was found at Dog Holes at Warton, and is now preserved in Lancaster City Museum.

The tribes which evolved from their mixing with the native population in the area formed a rich cultural heritage over the next two thousand years and from their fertile minds developed a host of 'magical' religious activity. Many of Lancashire's sacred sites, tales of the supernatural, and colourful customs began to evolve at this period. Earlier fertility cults now gave way to 'skyward' beliefs; the sun, the moon and the stars seem to have formed the basis of their religion, but in truth little is known of their rituals. But what remains in Lancashire from this period is a fascinating legacy of stone circles and ritual burial sites which contain the cremated remains of their leaders.

However, there is some evidence that both human and animal sacrifice may have been part of their beliefs. When Preston Dock was being excavated in 1885, thirty human skulls, sixty pairs of red deer antlers and forty ox skulls were uncovered, together with two dug-out canoes. This may have been a sacrificial site dating from between 2000BC and 500BC.

Sacred Sites

Evidence of the lost gods of Lancashire is still to be found on many windswept moorland hilltops and in the weathered stone remains which have been taken to the safety of our museums. Standing alone in these lonely places, steeped in the legends of a forgotten age of mysticism, it is tempting to speculate on what strange rites were once practised on these former sacred sites. Was it here that our ancestors bowed before the great Mother Goddess of Fertility? Did they worship the spirits of their dead ancestors, or perhaps stand in both fear and reverence before the great Sun God which lay at the basis of so many primitive religions? We will probably never know all the answers to the puzzle, yet the lure of these wild places remain as a rich legacy from our half-forgotten past.

A Druid High-Priest in Celtic Lancashire

One of the most intriguing of these sites is the Bleasdale Circle which stands in the shadow of wild Fair Snape Fell, six miles east of Garstang. Part-hidden in a woodland glade, it bathes in a marvellous atmosphere of timelessness that sweeps away all vestiges of modern Lancashire.

This early Bronze Age burial place, a wood-henge, dates from around 1900BC and was first excavated at the end of the last century. It was found to contain circles made from massive oak posts and birch poles, the latter lying flat in a ditch. Two funeral urns containing cremated human remains were uncovered within the inner circle. This construction, known as a palisaded barrow, is similar to others found in Europe, but none of these contained the original timber. The wooden posts were removed from the site and taken to the Harris Museum, being replaced with concrete replicas which still mark

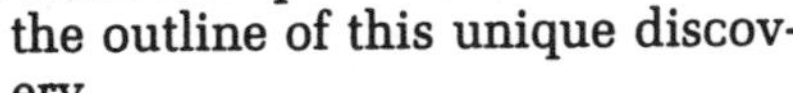

the outline of this unique discovery.

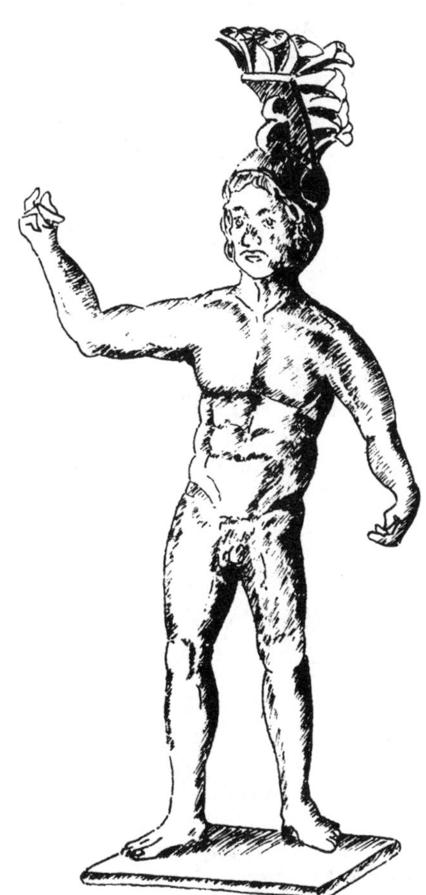

Mars, one of a host of Roman gods

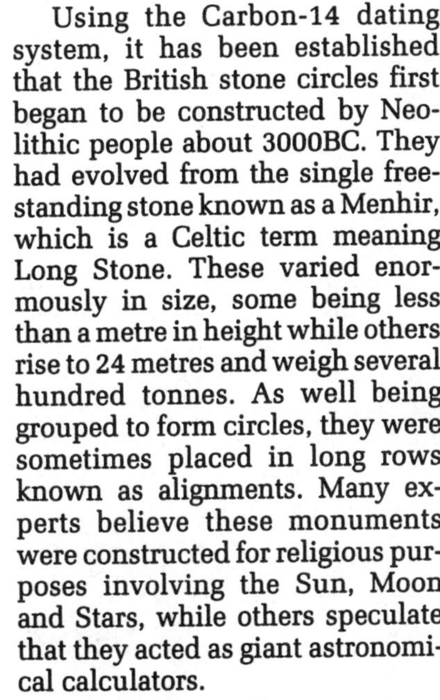

Using the Carbon-14 dating system, it has been established that the British stone circles first began to be constructed by Neolithic people about 3000BC. They had evolved from the single free-standing stone known as a Menhir, which is a Celtic term meaning Long Stone. These varied enormously in size, some being less than a metre in height while others rise to 24 metres and weigh several hundred tonnes. As well being grouped to form circles, they were sometimes placed in long rows known as alignments. Many experts believe these monuments were constructed for religious purposes involving the Sun, Moon and Stars, while others speculate that they acted as giant astronomical calculators.

The Calder Stones, six megaliths which are inscribed with elaborate spiral patterns, can be seen in Liverpool. They are thought to symbolise creation but during the 16th century, at which time only three had been discovered, they were used as boundary stones. However, their significance was later realised by archaeologists who now believe they once formed part of a passage grave, dating from 2500BC.

The former Furness district of Lancashire is rich in prehistoric links, having over 60 ancient sites. These include Swinside Stone Circle near Broughton-in-Furness which is known locally as the Sunken Kirk. It contains 52 stones and measures 27metres (88ft) in diameter. On Birkrigg Common, near Ulverston, can be found the romantically named Druid's Temple. Further south on the peaty plateau of Turton Heights, within the West Pennine Moors, stands another small stone circle. Lying close to the high point of Cheetham Close, it is believed to have formed part of a Bronze Age village. During Victorian times it was seriously vandalised to try to prevent local occultists using the mystical spot to practise their black art.

There are several other ritual burial sites within the West Pennine Moors which also seem to be surrounded by a lingering atmosphere of the supernatural. Anglezarke Moor, the name is of Irish-Norse origin, has at its very heart Lancashire's largest tumulus, Round Loaf. This massive protruding mound has never been officially excavated but has suffered from many an unofficial attempt. Set in a bowl of brown hills overlooking nearby Devil's Dyke, this lonely spot exudes an unnerving feeling of paganism. So it is not surprising that it is said to be favoured by modern witchcraft covens.

Just a few miles away across a sea of windswept moorland rises the sharp profile of Noon Hill. Perched on the edge of Rivington Moor at 1250feet (381metres) above sea level, it is one of the least visited summits in the area. This is perhaps because of it sinister reputation as being the abode of a spectral headless horseman. During the 17th century it was the meeting place of both Protestants and Nonconformists, who held their outlawed religious services away from prying eyes. But in 1958 the hilltop at last gave away its ancient secret for archaeologists uncovered a burial urn which contained cremated human remains which dated from 1100BC. These are now displayed in Bolton Museum.

Two Lads Hill

It is believed by some that the mystery of Lancashire's pagan past cannot be unravelled merely by identifying ritual sites, for it is necessary to also read the surrounding landscape. The shape of hilltops, the shadow cast by the sun at certain seasons, the embracing views from high vantage-points and the relationship between adjacent sites, all seem to be part of the rich equation. Our primitive ancestors lived close to the earth, and like blind people of today who develop amazing senses of hearing and touch, they could interpret secrets of the landscape which have become lost to modern man. So hidden among the high fells of Bowland, the splendid isolation of Pendle

Mysterious Two Lads Hill in the West Pennine Moors

and the windswept wilderness of Blackstone Edge may lie the clues from which we will one day rediscover our ancient heritage.

One man who has devoted a great deal of time attempting to uncover the fascinating history of one Lancashire hill is Robin Smith who lives at Great Lever, near Bolton. His mission began one hot summer's day in 1985 when he climbed to the attractive summit of Two Lads Hill on Wilder's Moor, which overlooks Horwich. While sitting among the piles of tumbled stones which are strewn around the hilltop, he became captivated by the lonely landscape. The windswept moorland had cast an irresistible spell: he became filled with an overwhelming desire to delve into the mystery of the hill.

His research led him to the works of such local historians as Thomas Hampson, John Albinson and Dorning Ramsbotham who in 1787 wrote the oldest account of the hill. A drawing from this period shows a circular wall about 17.7 metres (58ft) in diameter and 1.2 metres (4ft) high with a single gap 4.6metres (15ft) wide. This gap served as an entrance to the Two Lads, which were two large cairns measuring 2.4 metres (8ft) at their base, and standing 2 metres (6ft) apart.

One explanation for the structure that Robin's research revealed concerns Bishop Pilkington, a local man who lived during the 16th century and became the first Protestant Bishop of Durham. The story is that his two sons died in a snowstorm on Wilder's Moor and the cairns were constructed as their memorial. But Robin believes that if this were the case, then much more would have been written about such a tragic event, so it is unlikely to be true. Another similar tale states that the cairns cover the bodies of two sons of a Saxon king, whose parents had died in battle. And there does seem to be Saxon connections with the moorland for famous Winter Hill was once known as Edgar Hill, perhaps relating to King Edgar who is said to have hunted in the area. However, it is likely that the history of this mysterious hilltop goes back even further for there is evidence that it was an Iron Age hill fort built on the earlier site of a Bronze Age twin-cairn burial.

In his quest to find the truth Robin dug down to the base of the site, which he discovered was expertly built on a foundation of solid rock. He then reconstructed the cairns from the scattered stones, and with great feeling he skilfully restored them to their 18th-century splendour. But this brought him into conflict with the local authority which, to his consternation, sent workmen to the isolated site to demolish the structure which he had built with such care. However, this setback did not deter Robin. With determination his research into the puzzle of Two Lads Hill continues; perhaps our forgotten ancestors who worshipped their gods on Wilder's Moor want their secrets to be revealed.

Mysterious Stones

The highest land point in Lancashire is remote Gragareth, a wild hillside which forms part of Leck Fell, situated to the north-east of the village of Cowan Bridge. Just below the summit of the 2057 feet mountain stand three prominent cairns which have become known as the Three Men of Gragareth. Little is known about the origin of these structures, which today are used by walkers as welcome landmarks. But perhaps like the Two Lads cairns of the West Pennine Moors, they mark one of the sacred sites of Bronze Age man and are worthy of close investigation.

Curious legends which at first glance seem fanciful, are also often a clue to ancient sites. Towering above the impressive moorland valley of Cliviger Gorge near Burnley stands Eagle Crag, a lonely spot associated with witchcraft and ghosts. Here it is reputed lie the remains of Lady Sybil, wife of Lord William Towneley and a practitioner of the black-art. Black Rock, at the Mersey estuary, is traditionally the place where two centuries ago a sailor fell in love with a beautiful mermaid. She had to return to the sea, but first pledged her love by giving him a ring, promising they would soon be united. Her bond was not for this world, however, within five days the mariner was dead: together they found everlasting life in heaven.

Tockholes is an ancient village near Blackburn which recently had to fight the approach of a new motorway which threatened its rural identity. Its modern church replaced a Victorian building, which in turn occupied a site which was probably sacred before the arrival of Christianity. In the church-

The magical Toches Stone at Tockholes village

yard, mounted on a large, oblong, stone plinth inscribed with details of its history, is the Toches Stone. This supports the remnants of the parish preaching cross which date from AD684. The stone is reputed to have magical powers, being closely associated with the ancient tribe which once inhabited this valley, possibly when Tockholes was part of Brigantia. The closeness of the preaching cross indicates how a pagan site was turned into a place of Christian worship.

In 1963 a Bronze Age burial site was discovered at Astley Farm, Chorley, and was excavated in the 1970s. This yielded up a wealth of fascinating objects including burial urns and the cremated remains of at least six people. One small quartzitic sandstone pebble was of particular significance for it was identified as the tip of a phallus. This suggests that the religious rituals carried out during the burial were part of our ancient fertility beliefs.

Whalley, an attractive Ribble Valley village popular with visitors, has been a settlement since prehistoric times. Close to the present centre stands Portfield Camp, an Iron Age hill fort which dates back to 2000BC. Here the Celtic gods would have been worshipped over tens of centuries until the light of Christianity finally arrived. In the Anglo-Saxon Chronicle of AD664 it is known as Paegnalaech, the site of a monastery. Evidence of its Viking links can be seen in its three remarkable crosses which stand in the churchyard. The earliest one, which dates from the 11th century, shows the Norse symbol of eternity, the Dog of Berser.

To the north of the county rises majestic Warton Crag whose precipitous cliffs hide another Iron Age hill fort, while at the church of St Wilfred at nearby Halton can be seen a series of marvellous Anglo-Danish 11th-century crosses. But perhaps Lancashire's most impressive Viking link is the hog-backed tombstone which is housed within the church of St Peter at Heysham, overlooking the pounding waves of Morecambe Bay. It probably once marked the burial place of an important Viking warrior, its ornate inscriptions depicting Scandinavian legends from a pagan past.

Liverpool City Museum is the envy of the rest of Britain for its possession of the finest collection of Pagan Saxon antiquities in the country. Bought by a Liverpool collector during the last century, it contains unique examples of magnificent jewellery from the Dark Ages.

Pendle Hill

Writers and artists and walkers have for centuries been attracted by the magic of Pendle Hill. With awe and anticipation they climb its steep flank, then when at last they reach its windswept summit they are rewarded with one of England's finest views. But below them unfolds much more than a green landscape, wild and beautiful as it surely is; for Pendle Hill is an enigma. As the cold, grey mist creeps across its peaty plateau it is easy to let the imagination drift back into our past for this Lancashire hillside still echoes with memories of our pagan ancestors.

Seen from the splendour of the Ribble Valley, which lies on its western side, the hill resembles a huge brown whale that seems somehow to have become marooned in a sea of green meadowland. Its summit reaches a height of 1827 feet above sea level, just short of the 2000 feet mark which would classify it as a mountain. However, standing alone as it does with no other hills to compare it with, it gives the impression of being much higher. This has given rise to the saying:

Pendle Hill, Ingleborough and Penyghent,
Highest hills between Scotland and Trent.

Lying close to the border with Yorkshire, it is encircled by attractive villages and hamlets which sleep in sheltered hollows. Pendleton, Worston and Downham nestle to the west, with Barley, Newchurch and Sabden lying in the ancient Forest of Pendle to the east. Detached from the main Pennine range, the series of windswept moorlands which contain the hill rise gradually upwards for six miles from Whalley to reach the impressive Big-End, then plunge dramatically to the valley below. Varying between one and three miles wide, the hill is cut by several rugged cloughs, the horseshoe shaped Ogden Clough, which starts at Barley, being the largest.

The surface of Pendle is mainly rough moorland grass with areas of peat laid bare by the wind. Below lies hard millstone grit, which in turn rests upon a hidden bed of limestone. Over the centuries this mixture of soft and hard rock has led to an odd phenomenon which has become known locally as a water brast. It is believed to be caused by a build up of water pressure within the limestone core which becomes too strong to be contained by the gritstone so bursts through to the surface. The torrent of water then flows irresistibly down the hillside, sweeping away anything in its path. The last major water brast occurred in 1870, and others have been recorded in 1669 and 1580.

There is evidence to suggest that man has been seeking a god on Pendle Hill for thousands of years. This comes in the form of legends, place names and tales handed down from one generation to the next. Along the wild ridge which descends from Pendle summit towards Whalley is a high point with the curious name of Jeppe Knave Grave. Legend tells us that Jeppe, who lived during the early Norman period, was a criminal who broke the strict forest laws and paid with his life. At first the villagers of both Pendleton and Wiswell would not accept responsibility for his burial. However, eventually a compromise was reached and he was buried on the summit of the hill which lay exactly on the border between the two villages. But it is now believed that Jeppe Knave Grave is really a Bronze Age burial mound which, although plundered over the centuries, probably contained the remains of the leader of a local tribe. The site would have been of great religious significance to the people of this period, so perhaps the legend of Jeppe is an embellished folk tale with origins stretching back many thousands of years.

The steep winding road which now links Sabden to Clitheroe cuts across the southern flank of Pendle Hill at a point known as the Nick o' Pendle. Once filled with strings of packhorses, this was the historic route into the Forest of Pendle. It is overlooked by windswept Apronful Hill which is the subject of another local folk tale. This tells how a giant named Owd Nick (often the nickname of the Devil) took rocks from his apron then, while standing on this hilltop, hurled them at Clitheroe Castle. He managed to knock a hole in the keep wall but the effort broke his apron string, scattering his rocks on the ground where they still remain. He then escaped down the hillside to Deerstones Quarry, where his footprint can be seen embedded in a rock, before seeking the sanctity of Hameldon Hill which is situated six miles to the south. This tale, told for generations around the firesides of the Ribble Valley to amuse the children, may also have its foundation in the distant past – Owd Nick hurling his rocks representing the last gasp of paganism which was being driven out by Christianity. This may identify Apronful Hill as one of the ancient sacred sites where the 'Old Faith' was practised.

In this country there are numerous traditions associated with springtime, and particularly with May Day. Many of these can be traced back to the Celtic festival of Beltane or the worship of the Roman goddess Flora. In the Christian calendar May is known as Mary's Month, being attributed to the Virgin Mary, known to Roman Catholics as Our Lady. When the eminent travel writer H.V. Morton came to climb Pendle Hill in 1928, he found evidence of one of these traditions which he recorded in his book *The Call of England*. A local countryman who had lived in the area all his life spoke of the 'Springers' who came to the hill in large numbers prior to the First World War. Following in the footsteps of their pagan ancestors they would pass through the villages singing, then at midnight they began the climb to the summit of the hill. He believed they lit fires on the hilltop, then facing east they would await the rising of the sun on what was the first Sunday in spring.

Perhaps equally ancient as this reminder of sun worship is the now almost forgotten Robin Hood's Well which lies close to the top of the Big End. This is just one of many ancient sites in England which bear the name of the outlaw hero of Sherwood Forest. However, most of these are not directly associated with Robin Hood, but probably acquired the name when ballads about his exploits became popular in the 14th century. In the case of Pendle's elevated well the name may have changed from that of the Celtic hero, Robin Goodfellow. This suggests that it is likely to be a remnant of another pagan tradition, the worship of water spirits.

Bede tells us that many of these pagan sites were slowly transformed into places of Christian worship, and it seems that Robin Hood's Well was one of these. It is believed that a round-headed stone cross once stood alongside the well which, as a holy well, became a place of pilgrimage. At Easter the site attracted crowds of people from the surrounding towns of Burnley, Colne and Clitheroe. Many still climb Pendle Hill on Good Friday where a Christian service is held, but the well is now largely forgotten.

The Old Faith

The origins of what has now become known as witchcraft stretch like a thread into the mists of time. There is evidence to suggest that its roots lie deep in the pagan veneration of the Mother Goddess of the Stone Age. This ancient cult, in which the female body was revered as a symbol of fertility, continued over thousands of years. Its many forms spread throughout Europe and the Middle East, becoming part of the religious beliefs of the great civilizations of Egypt, Greece and Rome. But by this time a darker side to the Mother Goddess began to emerge. No longer was she merely revered as a divine life-giving force, but she began to be feared for her power of magic, sorcery and evil. Her power became even more threatening when she was given a menacing male consort in the form of a horned god.

The mythology surrounding the Mother Goddess and the Horned God became entwined with the pagan beliefs of the Celts then emerged in Europe as witchcraft. The term 'witch' having evolved from the Anglo-Saxon word 'wicca' which means 'the wise ones', referring to the many secrets, both good and evil, which followers of the cult were believed to hold.

A general belief that witches were responsible for many of the problems of the day continued over the centuries. The horrors of the witchhunt, in which alleged members of the cult were mercilessly persecuted, ebbed and flowed in its intensity throughout Europe. A Papal Bull had been issued in

The menacing Horned God, consort of the Mother Goddess

1484 condemning the practise and new laws were passed in Elizabethan England to further strengthen the fight against their 'miraculous works'.

But it was an incident which happened in 1590 in the small town of North Berwick on Scotland's east coast, that was to spark off a new English witch-hunt. It is said that in an empty church a group of witches gathered together to perform a hideous ritual involving the dismembered corpse of a man and the remains of a cat which had been cruelly tortured. They tossed their horrific sacrifice into the sea, which immediately responded by lashing into a great storm. One ship which was passing down the coast on its way to Leith was sunk by the heavy waves and many of its crew were drowned, but another vessel, which had been the real target of the witches' ritual, was more fortunate. This was a royal vessel that was carrying King James VI of Scotland from Denmark, and it managed to ride out the storm.

However, the news that witches had attempted to kill the King quickly spread though the country. An investigation followed which eventually led to almost seventy people from Edinburgh being accused of involvement in the plot. Eventually four witches were executed and James became convinced that the witches really possessed evil powers and intended to kill him. Being of a scholarly nature, he later wrote down his observations about the cult which were published in 1597 as *Demonology*.

In 1603, when he became the new king of England, he introduced harsher laws condemning those who carried out the secret rituals and his subjects were told to be ever-alert for practitioners of the black art. This royal nod of disapproval led to a terrible witchhunt which swept through England, reaching its horrific climax in the shadow of Pendle Hill.

The Pendle Witches

It was early in 1612, just nine years after King James I came to the throne, that the drama of the Pendle Witches slowly began to unfold. Its main characters were members of two poor and locally detested families named Demdike (Southern) and Chattox (Whittle).

Mother (Owd) Demdike, whose real name was Elizabeth Southern, was the head of her family. She was about eighty years old, blind, and due to her spiteful ways, was both feared and resented around Pendle Forest. Her home was Malkin Tower, which stood near Lower Well Head Farm, close to the village of Newchurch-in-Pendle. It is believed to have been demolished shortly after the witch trials, but the foundations of the building were still visible in 1900. It may have been part of a Norman pele Tower, built to protect the local people from the raiding Scots.

With Owd Demdike lived her widowed daughter, a hideously deformed and depraved woman named Elizabeth Device (nicknamed Squintin' Lizzie), and her three children, Alizon, James and Jennet. Alizon Device was said to be wild and emotional, James was mentally retarded, and Jennet was a precocious child of nine. Owd Demdike also had an illegitimate son named Christopher Holgate who lived locally with his wife, Elizabeth.

The Chattox family, who were deadly enemies of the Demdikes, lived in a hovel at Greenhead near the village of Fence, which is about two miles from Newchurch. Their leader was Anne Whittle who was known as Chattox, a nickname derived from her maiden name of Chadwick. Like her rival, she, too, was about eighty, almost blind and of a repulsive appearance. She lived with her two daughters, Elizabeth (Bessie) Whittle and Anne Redfearn, and Anne's husband, Thomas Redfearn.

The rivalry between the two families intensified during the 1600s when Bessie Whittle broke into Malkin Tower and stole some food and clothing. She was later seen by Alizon Device who recognised the stolen clothing she was wearing. A complaint was made to the local Justice of the Peace, Roger Nowell of Read Hall, who examined Bessie and then sent her for a period to Lancaster Castle Gaol. This was probably when the claim and counter-claim of witchcraft was first made by the two warring families.

But it was an event that happened on the 18th March 1612 that really brought the matter to a head. Alizon Device, who was going begging to Trawden, met a Halifax packman named John Law on the road near Colne. She asked him for some pins but he refused to open his pack, so she began to curse him. Fearful, he fell to the ground, paralysed by a stroke, with the lasting vision of a black dog with fiery red eyes in his mind. He was carried to a nearby ale house and his son, Abraham, later came over to tend him and investigate the incident.

On hearing the details, Abraham Law brought Alizon Device over to see his stricken father and, full of remorse, she asked for forgiveness for her deed. But Abraham, still seeking justice, reported her to the authorities. This led to her appearance before Roger Nowell at Read Hall on the 30th March 1612, accompanied by her mother Elizabeth and brother James. Under interrogation she readily confessed to being a witch, stating that the black dog was a devil spirit known as a familiar. She also told how her grandmother, Owd Demdike, had initiated her into the cult and that the whole Chattox family were witches. As a result Alizon Device was detained in custody.

Three days later, on the 2nd April 1612, Nowell continued his examinations at Ashlar House in Fence. Here Owd Demdike told how the Devil had first appeared to her at Newchurch in the guise of a boy named Tibb. He later changed into a dog who sucked blood from her body. Then with Tibb's assistance, she had brought about the death of Richard Baldwin's child as an act of revenge as he owed her daughter some money. Not to be outdone, Chattox then also confessed, saying how she had been initiated into the cult by Owd Demdike fourteen years before and had a familiar named Fancie. Many other witnesses than gave damning evidence which resulted in Owd Demdike, Chattox, Alizon Device and Anne Redfearn being sent to the dungeons of Lancaster Castle to await trial, charged under the 1604 Witchcraft Act.

But six days later on Good Friday, rumours began to spread that a Witches' Sabbat had been held at Malkin Tower. It was said that a large number of witches had gathered to consider freeing their accused colleagues from Lancaster Gaol. Evidence in the form of clay charms and human teeth were found, which was sufficient once more to alert the authorities.

On 27th April 1612 another examination of alleged witches was made by Roger Nowell and fellow magistrate Nicholas Bannister. They interrogated Owd Demdike's daughter, Elizabeth Device, her son James and her daughter Jennet. Accusations and confessions came fast and furious, these included tales of ritual murder and the implication of a wealthy gentlewoman, Alice Nutter of Roughlee Hall. The examination ended with Elizabeth and James Device, John and Jane Bulcock, Katherine Hewitt, Alice Grey and Alice Nutter being sent to Lancaster to join the others in the dank dungeons beneath the Well Tower. Another of the accused, Jennet Preston who lived at Gisburn, was sent to York for trial. But before the Lancaster trial got underway the main character, Owd Demdike, cheated the executioner by dying in her cell of natural causes.

The Pendle brood were not the only ones awaiting trial at the August assizes for the witch craze had now reached other parts of Lancashire. They had been joined by Isobel Robey of Windle near St Helens, Margaret Pearson of Padiham, and seven others from Samlesbury near Preston. Margaret Pearson had a particularly unsavoury reputation, having managed to cheat the gallows on two previous occasions, and was now being accused of murder by witchcraft.

The trials, held before Sir Edward Bromley and Sir James Altham, began on the 17th August 1612. Roger Nowell continued his role as Prosecutor, Thomas Potts of London acted as clerk of the Court, and incredibly by modern standards, none of the accused had defence lawyers! Chattox, who was accused of causing the death of Robert Nutter in 1595, was the first in the dock. She pleaded not guilty but unfortunately she had previously made a voluntary confession of guilt to Roger Nowell. The deformed Elizabeth Device next faced the judges, charged with three murders and facing damning evidence by her own young daughter, Jennet. One by one the others followed, telling their weird stories to an astonished court. Alice Nutter was perhaps the most puzzling of all for being wealthy and of a gentle nature she seemed to be a most unlikely witch, yet none of her family spoke in her defence. It now seems likely that she was really involved in the outlawed Roman Catholic faith, but somehow became wrongly implicated with witchcraft.

At the end of the two-day trials, nine of the Pendle Witches, together with Isobel Robey, heard the judge speak the terrible words, 'You shall go hence, to the castle from whence you came, from thence you shall be carried to the place of execution for this county, where your bodies shall be hanging until dead. And God have mercy upon your souls.'

They were executed on the 20th August 1612 on Gallows Hill, above Lancaster. The seven Samlesbury Witches were more fortunate in being acquitted, and Margaret Pearson for a third time escaped death. She was sentenced to stand in the pillory on market days, at Clitheroe, Whalley and Lancaster, then serve a one-year term in prison.

The saga of the Pendle Witches was written down in great detail in 1612 by the clerk, Thomas Potts, in *The Wunderfull Discoverie of Witches in the Countie of Lancaster*. This was republished in 1845 by the Chetham Society, which gave Victorian writer William Harrison Ainsworth the idea to write a novel based on the true story. After spending time at Newchurch and Whalley, where he stayed at Bridge House, his best-selling *The Lancashire Witches* appeared in 1848. Over a century later, in 1953, Robert Neill wrote a modern version, *Mist Over Pendle*, which was also well received. Then in recent years a host of other books have followed, exploring all the facets of this sad episode in our history.

Chapter Five

Christian Magic

The New Faith

During the early years of the first century, while the Celts of Lancashire were honouring their goddess Brigantia, at the eastern end of the Roman Empire the new faith of Christianity was beginning to take hold. Less than twenty years after Christ died on the cross, all the main centres of the Roman Empire, from Alexandria to Rome, had groups of followers of the new religion. But how Christianity first arrived in Britain is a matter of speculation. One well-known legend relates that the young Jesus actually came here with his uncle, Joseph of Arimathea, which resulted in our first Christian church being built at Glastonbury in Somerset. However, the earliest evidence of an active Christian community in this country comes from a fragment of pottery discovered in Manchester. Dating from the late 2nd century, it is inscribed with coded letters which when re-arranged read 'Our Father'.

By this time England was part of the Roman Empire, but Christianity flourished only as a semi-secret organisation. To the Romans the cult members were seen as possible troublemakers who venerated an 'executed criminal' and declared that there was only one true God, refusing to acknowledge the divinity of the Emperor.

It was almost four centuries before Christianity really triumphed in Lancashire, but even after this time the old gods were never completely forgotten. During this period the persecution of Christians led to many of them dying for their faith, which in turn led to these martyrs themselves becoming subjects of veneration.

A break in the progress of Christianity came when the Anglo-Saxons swept through the country, eventually reaching Brigantia and forcing the Britons to retreat to remote isolation. Crushed by Tiw, Woden and other gods, the light of Christianity was almost, but not quite extinguished. This became a period of spiritual pessimism, for the Anglo-Saxons were gloomy fatalists who believed that only fame in this world was important.

However, by the mid-sixth century the isolation of the Celtic church ended and its missionaries began to progress into what was then Northumbria, later to be joined by St Augustine's mission from Rome. At Winwick church a Celtic wheel cross is a legacy from this period, for here it is said died the Saxon King Oswald of Northumbria. He was a Christian and in conflict with his pagan neighbour, Penda of Mercia. Further evidence of the restoration of Christianity can be seen in the unique ruins of St Patrick's Chapel on the cliff edge at Heysham, together with six rock-hewn graves.

In the early churches the bodies of saints were often buried beneath the altar and these became places of pilgrimage. By the 9th century it had become common practice for people to carry around with them relics of saints for personal veneration, often encapsulated in a ring or brooch. Pilgrims made long treks to the great cathedrals and monasteries to gaze upon the bodies of these holy men and to pray at their tombs for favours.

At Chorley the skull and thigh bones of St Lawrence were given to the church by Sir Rowland Standish of Duxbury to become highly-prized relics. Beneath the altar of the Sodality Chapel in Stonyhurst College are the bones of St Gordianus, a martyr from the early Roman church which flourished in the catacombs. A leather-bound, hollow cross kept at Whalley is said to contain part of the swaddling-clothes of the infant Jesus, while a room at the Shrine of our Lady of Fernyhalgh near Preston contains one of England's finest collection of relics. These include part of the hair shirt worn by St Thomas More, dust from the tomb of St Francis and a measure of Our Lady's foot taken from her sandal which is kept in Spain.

The turmoil following King Henry VIII's break with Rome during the 16th century led to the creation of a whole group of locally-born martyrs. The following 150 years brought an unparalleled period of religious persecution. The soil of Lancashire became tragically stained with the blood of Catholics, Protestant and non-conformists; all Christians fighting for the right to worship according to their conscience.

Magical Sites

Paganism was widespread within Anglo-Saxon Lancashire until the early 7th century when Celtic monks from Iona, under the leadership of St Aidan, began their missionary work in Northumbria. They had been invited by the Christian King Oswald in 634, making their base on Holy Island. However, when Oswald was killed by the heathen King Penda of Mercia in AD642, the new faith faced a severe setback. The battle is said to have taken place at Winwick, where the church is now dedicated to the saintly King. His dismembered body was then taken to Mercia to be displayed at Oswestry, which means Oswald's Tree. A later attempt to convert the northern pagans was made by St Paulinus who came from the south as a missionary of the Roman church. But although he made rapid progress, probably visiting Lancashire, much of his work was not lasting for in 732 Northumbria returned to worshipping the old gods.

However, when the new faith eventually became established the early churches were often built on sites considered magical by the former pagans. Many of these ancient churches in Lancashire stand on ley lines, and have traditions and legends which link them to the old beliefs. The oldest Christian buildings still in use in the county are believed to be St Helen's church at Overton, which nestles close to the Lune estuary, and the nearby clifftop church of St Peter at Heysham. While the Runic stone and incised cross at St Luke's church at Formby, known as the God Stone, indicates what was once a pagan site.

The site of Colne Church was chosen by supernatural intervention

Colne parish church is one of many scattered throughout England on a site said to have been chosen by supernatural intervention. The original site of the first church was intended to be at Church Clough, about half a mile from the present building, but every stone laid by the masons by day was carried at night by 'unseen hands' and laid at the present site. Eventually, the builders were forced to take notice of the omen, erecting the building as dictated by the mystical forces. The event is remembered by the rhyme:

This church will ne'er be built aright,
Up in the day, down in the night.
Build it upon old Colne Hill,
And at Judgement Day 'twill be there still.

It has also been found that the church does not lie on the traditional East-West line. One explanation for this is that it was built to face the place on the horizon where the sun rose on the morning of the Patron Saint's Day (St Bartholomew). However, both the mysterious tale of the siting of the church together with its unusual alignment may well have more ancient links, perhaps lying in an uneasy compromise between Christianity and paganism. Other Lancashire churches which are also reputed to have been mysteriously moved from their chosen sites, include St Chad's at Rochdale, Newchurch in Rossendale and Leyland parish church.

Halton, an ancient village which lies on the banks of the River Lune, just three miles from Lancaster, has a church with a fascinating history. The present building, dedicated to St Wilfred, is mainly Victorian with some original Norman features. However, a series of cross shafts which have survived point to the site having once been sacred to the old gods. In the churchyard stands a carved cross which is unique in Britain, depicting on its east and north face a pagan legend, and on the west face Christian scenes. Dating from about AD1000 the cross is Norse, telling the legendary story of Sigurd. Other cross parts within the church are even older, being Anglo-Saxon dating from AD800. But a fine stone altar found in the village and once used by the Romans to worship their gods was claimed by the British Museum.

The dedication of the church to St Wilfred, together with those at Ribchester and Standish, suggests that they may all have been founded by this holy man about AD680. A local holy well dedicated to the saint and now almost forgotten may also be a link to the time when water spirits demanded their sacrifice. The miraculous water, once used to cure eye ailments, is remembered by the verse:

O come with us to St Wilfred's Well,
Its waters carry a kindly spell;
Bathe your eyes and the charm will be
That you with clearer sight shall see.

Prominent above the church is a large mound which marks the site of a motte and bailey castle. A local tradition states that the wayward brother of King Harold, Earl Tostig, lived here and was buried on the site after he was killed at the Battle of Stamford Bridge near York. Both Harold and Tostig claimed descent from the Norse Sigurd shown on the cross.

In the library at Stonyhurst College in the Ribble Valley is a 7th-century copy of the Gospel of St John which was carried by St Cuthbert during his lifetime and buried with him in AD686. This great saint became better known after his death than during his lifetime as monks carried his body and the head of St Oswald throughout Northumbria for seven years in order to elude the pagan Viking invaders who were attacking the east coast:

O'er northern mountain, marsh and moor,
From sea to sea, from shore to shore,
Seven years St Cuthbert's corpse they bore.

During the period from AD875 to 883, his dedicated disciples guarded his sacred relics. When they stopped for a short halt they built a cross, and when they stayed for a longer period a simple church was erected. Their wanderings brought them into Lancashire, where many of the ancient churches dedicated to St Cuthbert are believed to mark their stopping places. These include those at Aldingham in Furness, Over Kellet between Lancaster and Kendal, Lytham, Halsall and Churchtown, near Southport.

Wayside crosses, holy wells, local legends and place names are all pointers to the path of Lancashire's first missionaries. Filled with intense passion for their new faith, they wandered through our untamed northern countryside, willing to die rather than give up the fight to convert the pagan. The few we remember as saints, but many remain forgotten, their names erased by the passage of time.

Preston's Miraculous Cures

It is proudly boasted that the splendid white steeple of St Walburge's church, which dominates the skyline of Preston, is the third highest in all of England. Designed by Joseph Hansom, who gave his name to the hansom cab, this impressive building was consecrated in 1854. However, few people who gaze up in admiration at what has become a symbol of Proud Preston realise that behind its name lies the tale of not one, but three miraculous cures.

In the middle of the last century the town had witnessed a massive rise in its Catholic population to 20 000 parishioners, mainly poor, hard-working people. The three churches which served the expanding town were proving to be completely inadequate leading to severe overcrowding, so the Jesuit fathers decided that a new school and church were required. By collecting the pennies of the many it became possible in 1852 to open the first phase of the scheme, a small building named St Joseph's Chapel. It was also intended that the new church would carry the same name, but the mysterious events which were to follow changed all this.

Preston's miraculous cures had their origins in Saxon England. Saint

Walburge, the daughter of the King of Wessex, was born in 710, a member of a devout Christian family. She began her studies to become a nun at the age of only 10 when she entered a convent at Wimborne in Dorset. In 750 she went with her two brothers, who were also destined to become saints, to Germany where the great St Boniface was a missionary. There she completed her life's work, becoming the head of both a monastery and a convent.

After her death in 778 her body was taken to a convent in Eichstadt and placed in a bronze shrine which rested on a marble table. It was then found that each year between the 12 October and the anniversary of her death, the 25 February, a transparent moisture began to flow from the marble. This strange liquid, which was collected by the nuns in a silver vase, became known as Saint Walburge's Oil. Over the centuries tales of its unique properties grew, many believing that its application could result in miraculous cures from any ailment.

In 1853 Alice Holderness was working as a housemaid at St Wilfred's presbytery in Preston when she had a fall which broke her kneecap. Doctors treated her injury, but unfortunately the break would not heal and eventually they pronounced that it was incurable. However, a Jesuit named Father Norris had obtained a phial of St Walburge's Oil which he decided to apply to the housemaid's injury. An astonished eye-witness later recorded that 'the bones immediately snapped together and she was perfectly cured, having no longer the slightest weakness in the broken limb.'

News of the alleged miraculous cure swept through the town. Sceptics, including the editor of a local newspaper, poured scorn on the incident, but the Catholic clergy were convinced that a miracle had happened. It was then decided that it would be appropriate to dedicate the new church to St Walburge.

However, this was not the end of the affair for the following year another cure was attributed to the oil. Mary Meagher, a local girl, suffered from fits and convulsions which led to the inside of her mouth being badly gashed. Her mother persuaded Father Edward Swarbrick to apply the oil to the child and by the next morning she had been permanently healed. She grew up to marry and lead a normal life, remaining completely free from the affliction which had marred her early years.

The third cure, which occurred in 1858, involved a nun named Sister Walburga Bradley. Bedridden for five months by a serious stomach complaint which her doctor said was incurable, she was unable to take solid foods and was believed to be dying. The chaplain decided to apply Saint Walburge's Oil to her, gently placing a thread dipped in the liquid onto her tongue. Her instant recovery astonished her doctor who was not a Catholic, but prepared to accept that the oil had worked although he did not know how.

Since that time no further cures have been recorded using the oil in Preston, but at St Walburge's Shrine in Eichstadt plaques line the walls testifying to many similar miracles throughout the world.

The Holy Hand

Not even the mind of Sir Arthur Conan Doyle could have dreamed up a work of fiction to match the real life of Edmund Arrowsmith. This remarkable tale of a priest who was forced to act like a secret agent began in Elizabethan Lancashire and continues to this day. Following his bloody execution came a warning brought by an apparition, the veneration of his severed hand, many miraculous cures, the strange imprint of a cross in an ash tree, and finally the bestowing on this Lancashire man of the Roman Catholic Church's highest honour – sainthood. His story also links up three different parts of the county: Ashton-in-Makerfield near Wigan, the small village of Brindle which lies between Blackburn and Preston, and the ancient city of Lancaster.

It was in the village of Haydock, which lies a mile from Ashton-in-Makerfield, that Brian Arrowsmith (later confirmed Edmund) was born in 1585. His parents, Margery and Robert, were staunch Roman Catholics; not an enviable position to take at this period for their faith was outlawed and its members mercilessly persecuted. This became quickly apparent to Brian for when he was aged eight he witnessed a raid on the family home by the priest hunters, who were known as pursuivants. His parents were taken off to jail at Lancaster, and Brian, together with the three other Arrowsmith children, was left shivering in his night clothes. This would undoubtedly have been a traumatic episode which remained in his memory forever.

The holy hand of St Edmund Arrowsmith

Eventually Margery and Robert Arrowsmith were released after paying a fine, but his father then went abroad for a eriod to escape the terrible harassment. Sadly, shortly after his return to Haydock he died – an event which he had foretold.

In 1605, the same year as the Gunpowder Plot which increased hostility towards Catholics, Brian Arrowsmith sailed to the continent. He had made the decision to study for the priesthood at the English College at Douai. Confirmed with the name Edmund, he was finally ordained on the 9 December 1612 and returned as an undercover missionary priest to his native Lancashire in June 1613. His mission was centred on the village of Brindle, covering the countryside around Chorley, Clayton Green, Walton-le-dale and Samlesbury. A witty, scholarly man with an intense love for his faith, he carried out his clandestine activities for ten years.

His work brought him into contact with colleagues who were members of the intellectual Jesuit Order, often called the soldiers of Christ. Over the years he came to admire the fervent way in which they administered their duties and decided that he, too, would like to join the order. After a retreat in Essex, he was accepted into their ranks and his life became even more secretive.

At this time one hundred and thirty Jesuits were working in England, their territories being divided into regions they termed colleges. To escape detection they used a sophisticated system of code words. When they mentioned 'Mr Abraham' they were talking about the Pope, priests were called 'factors', and their college they called the 'factory'. Edmund Arrowsmith assumed the names Mr Bradshaw and Mr Rigby, and had his base at the ancient Blue Anchor Inn at Brindle.

The intensity with which the authorities pursued 'papists' varied over the years depending upon the political climate. In 1622 Edmund Arrowsmith was arrested and brought before the Bishop of Chester for examination. He was fortunate at this time for King James I was trying to arrange a marriage for his son, the future Charles I, with the King of Spain's daughter. To foster the right climate for the negotiations with the Catholic country the King ordered the release of many Catholic priests, so Edmund had a lucky escape.

However, in 1628 he was not so fortunate. He had a disagreement with the son of the landlord of the Blue Anchor Inn regarding the young man's marriage before a Protestant minister, which Edmund considered invalid. Furious over the affair, the young man reported the priest to the local Justice of the Peace, who although reluctant, was forced by the laws of the time to act. Edmund was warned that the priest hunters were about to arrive so he made his escape on horseback across Brindle Moss. Unfortunately, when he met a ditch which crossed the rough terrain his horse refused to jump, allowing the priest hunters to catch up with him. After a skirmish he was arrested then marched off to the Blue Boar Inn where they locked him in the cowshed. He was later transported to Lancaster Castle dungeons.

It was on the 26 August 1628 that Edmund Arrowsmith was brought to trial. The presiding judge was Henry Yelverton who had boasted that he would sentence to death all Catholic priests who came before him. Although King Charles I was by now married to his Catholic Queen, he had little power to exert his authority.

"Sir, are you a priest?" asked Yelverton.

"I would to God I were worthy," replied Arrowsmith, making the sign of the cross.

"Yes," the Judge answered, "though he is not, yet he desires to be a traitor; this fact makes him guilty. Are you no priest?"

The banter continued between the two, eventually reaching its inevitable conclusion when Edmund Arrowsmith was finally sentenced to death with the terrible words:

"You shall go from hence to the place from whence you came; from thence you shall go to the place of execution on a hurdle. You shall be hanged by the neck till you be half-dead; your members shall be cut off before your eyes and thrown into the fire, where likewise your bowels shall be burnt. Your head shall be cut off and set upon a pole, and your quarters shall be set upon the four corners of the Castle. And may God have mercy on your soul."

After receiving absolution from John Southworth of Samlesbury Hall, who himself was a prisoner at this time, Edmund Arrowsmith was taken to a hillside above Lancaster on the 28 August 1628 and the horrific execution took place. He died with the words, "Bone Jesu, Good Jesus," on his lips.

As his life slipped away two mysterious events are said to have taken place. The father of John Southworth told how he saw 'a very brilliant light extending in a luminous stream from the prison to the gallows like a resplendent glass'. And in another part of Lancashire a Benedictine monk named Ambrose Barlow was visited by an apparition of Edmund Arrowsmith who warned him, "I have suffered, and now you will be to suffer; say little, for they will endeavour to take hold of your words."

Following his death several relics of Edmund Arrowsmith were secured by his followers, the most famous one being his severed hand. This came into the possession of the Gerard family of Bryn who were relatives of his mother. Soon afterwards the hand became venerated by pilgrims, its application is believed to have resulted in numerous miraculous cures including those of Thomas Hawarden in 1726, Mary Fletcher in 1768 and Mary Selby in 1832.

On the 25 October 1970 Edmund Arrowsmith was one of forty martyrs who were canonized. Since 1822 his holy hand, which is now housed in St Oswald's Church at Ashton-in-Makerfield, has become the source of a weekly pilgrimage. Over 150 people attend the service and favours, including miraculous cures, are continually attributed to his intercession. Pieces of linen which have been in contact with the holy hand are also requested by people from all over the world.

At the isolated village of Brindle where the Saint carried out his ministry there are still many reminders of his presence. In St Joseph's Church the high altar is an ornately carved sideboard which was once used by him, and in the sacristy is preserved his tattered chasuble. On Gregson Lane stands a Tudor cottage known as the House of the Last Mass. A plaque over the door tells how he 'offered the sacrifice of the Mass in this house', and Mass is still celebrated regularly in an upstairs room. Other ancient homes in the area connected with him include Higher Shuttling Farm and Malt Kiln Farm which contains a cupboard where a chalice used to be hidden. The Blue Boar Inn, where he was once held prisoner, remains a popular hostelry.

A century ago an ancient cottage in Brindle was blown down in a gale and in the ruins were found a chalice, an altar stone and part of a vestment. This had an amazing sequel in 1983 when a parishioner, George Addison, was cutting down an ash tree which stood near the site of the cottage. As he split the wood it opened to reveal the distinct outline of a cross. The tree was believed to have been about 130 years old, so it is thought that the cross had been hidden there when the cottage had been destroyed and the wood had grown around it.

A Bloody Footprint

Perched on the edge of rising moorland three miles north-east of Bolton stands half-timbered Smithills Hall, one of Lancashire's finest manor houses. Its known history goes back to the 14th century when it was owned by the mysterious Knights Hospitallers, but the site is much older. Over the centuries seven different families have made it their home, including a branch of the ancient Radclyffes of Radclyffe Tower. However, this private ownership came to an end in 1938 when the last residents, the Ainsworth family, sold their impressive residence to Bolton Corporation. But with this fine building came a supernatural inheritance. Since the 16th century it has become widely known as the Hall of the Bloody Footmark due to a gruesome story concerning the life and death of a Protestant martyr.

George Marsh was a farmer's son who was born in 1515 at Deane, an ancient parish which lies close to Bolton. From an early age he became a keen student of the New Testament, wholeheartedly taking to the newly reformed religion which now had King Henry VIII as its head. In 1547, when he was 31 years old and the young Edward VI had acceded to the throne, he was appointed as a preaching minister. He travelled throughout Lancashire, spreading his personal belief in what he saw as being the Christian truth, based on the simple message of biblical texts.

In 1553 Edward VI died of tuberculosis and Lady Jane Grey became Queen for only nine days before being deposed and then succeeded by Queen Mary who was a fervent Roman Catholic. Immediately she revoked several Acts of Uniformity and began to re-establish the once outlawed faith, reviving the celebration of Mass, holy days, and the celibacy of priests. Protestants who opposed the new order now became the subject of savage persecution, as Catholics themselves had been just a few years earlier.

George Marsh now found himself caught up in this countrywide relig-

George Marsh's memorial cross in Deane churchyard, Bolton

ious witch-hunt. His mother and brother were both threatened, which led him to go voluntarily before magistrate Sir Roger Barton at Smithills Hall, accused of 'preaching false doctrines'. His trial took place in the upper Green Chamber, where a verdict of guilty was quickly announced. As he walked downstairs he was greeted by members of his family who implored him to renounce his stubborn beliefs. Unmoved by their pleas he refused, then with steadfast conviction he stamped his foot heavily down on the stone floor. As he did so he prayed that the footprint would remain as a permanent symbol of his terrible injustice.

Marsh faced further questioning before Lord Derby at Latham House, where he confirmed his beliefs. He was then imprisoned at Lancaster Castle where attempts were made to extract from him the names of his fellow Lancashire reformers, but this failed. Here his time was spent in pious prayer and Bible readings, which led to local people gathering outside his cell to listen. Angered by this, the authorities then moved him to Chester to be questioned yet again, this time by the new Bishop. Again he refused to abandon his interpretation of the bible, which ended with him being sentenced to the ultimate punishment. In April 1555 he was taken outside the city walls then chained to a stake before being horribly burnt to death.

However, the impression he made with his foot on the floor at Smithills Hall still remains as a poignant reminder. It varies in colour from dark brown to reddish blue, being more perceptible when washed. Once a prankster is said to have removed the slab from the floor, which led to a great supernatural upheaval in the house until it was replaced.

A few years ago members of a local history society visited the Victorian wing of the Hall and discovered another strange image. On the floor of the kitchen passage was the clear profile of a larger than life human face. Staff who work in the building related how sometimes it appears to be male, then at other times female. The historians then decided to take several photographs but astonishingly, when the films were developed and printed, all those which should have contained the face appeared blank, while other subjects remained quite normal!

Pendle Hill Vision

It was perhaps inevitable that George Fox, who was to become the great force behind the foundation of the Quaker movement, should be drawn to Pendle Hill. As he wandered through 17th- century England in search of spiritual enlightenment, tales of the supernatural reputation of Pendle must surely have reached his ears.

The son of a weaver, George Fox was born in 1624 at Fenny Drayton in Leicestershire. He became a shoemaker's apprentice, but from childhood had become absorbed by the question of religious belief. The teachings of his

Mysterious Pendle Hill where George Fox had a supernatural vision

day did not satisfy his enquiring mind so in 1643 he left home to begin what was to become a lifetime of wandering. His early quest was to seek out "the pure knowledge of God and Christ alone", then later he became a great preacher, intent on passing on his personal message to others.

His journal, which was first published in 1694, three years after his death, has become a religious classic. Recording his fascinating journey through both Europe and America, it also outlines the terrible persecutions and long terms of imprisonment that he had to endure.

In 1652 he and his colleague Richard Farnworth passed through Derbyshire and arrived in Lancashire. His journal then recorded:

'And the next day we passed on, warning people as we met them of the day of the Lord that was coming upon them. As we went I spied a great high hill called Pendle Hill, and I went on the top of it with much ado, it was so steep; but I was moved of the Lord to go atop of it; and when I came atop of it I saw Lancashire sea: and there atop of the hill I was moved to sound the day of the Lord; and the Lord let me see a-top of the hill in what places he had a great people to be gathered. As I went down, on the hill side I found a spring of water and refreshed myself, for I had eaten little and drunk little for several days.'

The enlightenment that George Fox found as he gazed out from the top of Pendle Hill became a milestone in his quest. This was eventually to lead to the foundation of the worldwide Society of Friends. The water which he drank is believed to have been from Robin Hood's Well, which is now also known as Fox's Well. In the United States the event is commemorated by the Friends' Pendle Hill Library at Wallingford, Pennsylvania.

Saint or Sinner?

The preservation of human heads is a practice which few would associate with modern Lancashire, yet, surprisingly, hidden away in some of our lesser known churches and ancient houses, are several of these links to a past age. The Celts of Brigantia began the practice as they placed great significance on the face and head, believing it possessed magical powers. But many of the preserved heads which remain today are religious relics of those who died for their faith.

Wardley Hall, which lies within the manor of Worsley on the outskirts of Manchester, is the home of the Roman Catholic Bishop of Salford. Here is preserved what is now believed to be the skull of Saint Ambrose Barlow, a priest who was martyred at Lancaster in 1641. However, for many years the skull was said to have been that of Roger Downes, a man who was anything but saintly for he had the reputation of being a hell-raising rake.

This impressive half-timbered building, which dates back to the 16th century, was built by the Tyldesley family then later came into the possession of the Downes. During the reign of Charles II the last of the male line was Roger Downes, a courtier in London who pursued a life of vice and corruption. It is said that one evening while out with his friends on a drunken binge, he was crossing London Bridge when he made a wager that he would kill the first person he met. The unfortunate victim was a tailor who Downes cut down, but his callous act was seen by a watchman who was the policeman of the period. In the fight which followed, the watchman struck at Downes with his razor-sharp bill, a blow finally decapitating the vicious thug. Some time later a box was delivered to Wardley Hall. To the horror of Downes's sister Maria, it was found to contain the severed head. This gruesome relic eventually found a permanent resting place close to the staircase within the house, but it was reputed that if anyone moved it evil disturbances followed.

However, it is now believed that the tale was created as a cover during a period of religious persecution, when the possession of such a relic could have brought the family's downfall. This theory was substantiated in 1729 when the Downes family vault was opened in Wigan Church. The body of Roger Downes was seen, complete with his head, although part of the skull had been removed, possibly for a post-mortem examination.

So the real owner of the skull seems to have been Ambrose Barlow who was born in 1585 at Barlow Hall near Manchester. One of fourteen children of a Catholic family, he found himself drawn to the outlawed religious life from an early age. This led him to take up training abroad, then after being ordained in 1615, becoming a Benedictine monk and returning to an undercover mission in his native Lancashire. Happily living in extreme poverty, he administered to the poor of Leigh, Ormskirk, Warrington and Liverpool; the latter at this time being only a small town.

In March 1641 the Long Parliament had warned all Catholic priests to leave Britain within one month, but Barlow, who was ill, chose to ignore the ruling. Shortly after celebrating Easter Mass he was arrested, then quickly transported to Lancaster for trial, guarded by sixty armed men. His defence, which stated that he was a Benedictine, not a Jesuit or seminary priest which were mentioned by the edict, failed. This resulted in him being sentenced to death by being hanged, drawn and quartered.

The noble monk accepted his fate with dignity by replying to the judge's claim that he was a 'seducer' with the words, "I am no seducer, but a reducer of people to the ancient religion." On the 10 September 1641 he was taken on a hurdle to Lancaster's place of execution above the town, carrying a simple wooden cross in his hand. He then walked three times around the scaffold reciting the miserere before the horrific punishment was carried out. His head and quarters were then displayed on the walls of Lancaster Castle and at the Collegiate Church in Manchester.

It is believed that his severed head was later acquired as a relic by one of his followers, then eventually taken to the security of Wardley Hall where he had once been a chaplain. It was to be a further 329 years before this holy man was given the mantle of sainthood in October 1970.

Martyr's Skulls

Mawdesley is a quiet village which lies to the south-west of Chorley. Surrounded by rich agricultural land and overlooked by the ruins of a windmill which is perched on nearby Harrock Hill, it presents a tranquil face. Yet within lovely Lane End House, a 16th-century building which lies on the edge of the village, hides a secret from a less peaceful period. A clue to its past is given by the name locals call the dwelling – Skull House. At the top of the building is a hidden chapel in which is kept a precious relic which is venerated by local Catholics: the skull of a martyr.

It is said to have belonged to William Haydock, a Cistercian monk of Whalley Abbey who opposed the suppression of the monasteries so became involved in the uprising known as the Pilgrimage of Grace. He was executed in 1536, but his skull was later obtained by his family who secretly kept it as a relic at their home, Cottam Hall in the Fylde. In the early 18th century a member of the family, Mary Haydock, married Thomas Finch and the couple came to live at the Finch family home at Mawdesley, bringing the relic with them. At the same time Mary's brother, Cuthbert, who was a priest, also came to live in the house and it was he who established the hidden chapel. Pilgrims came many miles to venerate the relic, often seeking miraculous cures from illnesses, and on occasions taking away teeth from the skull.

However, the Haydock family are also said to have had another martyr's skull in their possession, which seems to have been lost. This belonged to George Haydock who was working in London as an underground priest in 1582. He was betrayed to the priest hunters by a Fylde man named Hankinson, and thrown into the Tower dungeons. Later came his trial at Westminster Hall where he was condemned to death for high treason, then executed at Tyburn on the 12 February 1584, aged 27. Like his ancestor, William Haydock, his skull was obtained by the family then brought north to Cottam Hall where it was hidden in the chapel, but its location is now unknown.

The Gory Head of Mowbreck Hall is a tale concerning the prediction of the death of George Haydock. It began on Hallowe'en, the day preceding the arrest of the priest in London. At this time Vivian Haydock, the father of George Haydock, was at Mowbreck Hall on the Fylde, a house belonging to the Westby family who were related to the Haydocks of Cottam. Vivian was a priest who had taken holy orders in old age, following the death of his wife. The old man was robed in vestments at the altar when, as the clock struck midnight, a ghostly manifestation rose above him holding the severed head of his son. The sight so shocked him that he fell unconscious, never to recover, his body being later buried beneath the chapel at Cottam. Unexplained noises heard at ancient Mowbreck Hall during the 1960s, by which time it had become a restaurant, were said to be caused by the restless spirit of Vivian Haydock.

Catforth is another secluded part of the Fylde which holds secrets of a turbulent past. Visitors to lonely St Robert's Church are sometimes startled when they gaze behind a purple curtain that stands close to the altar. Sitting on a cushion alongside a chalice, vestments and a missal, rests a 400-year-old severed human head! In a remarkable state of preservation, the flesh and skin have become hardened by time, the jaw is slightly opened and it can be clearly seen where, halfway through the fifth vertebra, the head was hacked off.

For many years it was believed that the head was that of Father Philip Holden who was killed in 1648 by Cromwell's soldiers at Chaigley, in the Ribble Valley. However, after a painstaking investigation by J.E. Bamber, this has now been discounted. It is now believed that it belongs to Miles Gerard, a priest who was executed at Rochester, Kent, about 1590. His sister married into the Holden family, so it is likely that that is how they acquired the relic, which they kept secretly until 1823 when it was entrusted to St Robert's Church.

Chingle Hall near Preston has gained a national reputation in recent years for it is said to be the most haunted house in England. Ghost hunters flock in each year to investigate the host of unexplained happenings that have been recorded in the ancient hall. Strange noises, ghostly footsteps, objects being thrown through the air and even the apparition of a cowled monk are seen regularly. It is now thought by some that behind this weird catalogue of supernatural activity lies another severed head which is hidden within the building. This perhaps belongs to Saint John Wall whose spirit wishes the relic to be discovered.

He was born at Chingle Hall in 1620 during a period of religious persecution, to a family who originated from Norfolk. His baptism was carried out by the clandestine priest Edmund Arrowsmith who was also destined for sainthood. In 1645, after training at Douai and Rome, he was ordained a priest then later entered the order of Friars Minor of St Bonaventure's. His missionary work in England was based in Warwickshire and the surrounding counties where he ministered for 23 years.

But his activities came to an end in 1678, when he was discovered at the home of the Finch family at Harvington in Worcestershire. His trial, which even saddened many local Protestants, took place at Worcester, followed by his execution on the 22 August 1679. It is said that his body was buried at an unknown spot in St Oswald's Churchyard in Worcester. However, some people believe that his head was brought back for secret burial at his birthplace of Chingle Hall, and it is his apparition that is seen around the house.

The Southworths of Samlesbury were another distinguished Lancastrian family who greatly suffered for their adherence to the Catholic faith. Sir John Southworth, in spite of having been knighted for his bravery in fighting the

Scots in 1547 and becoming the Sheriff of Lancashire in 1562, would not flinch from his beliefs. He was later detained in prison at both Salford and Manchester for harbouring the Jesuit, Edmund Campion, at Samlesbury Hall.

But it is another member of the family, also named John, who has gained worldwide recognition – in 1970 it was announced that he was to become a saint and his preserved body, which lies in a shrine at Westminster Cathedral, has become a place of pilgrimage. He had been born at Samlesbury Hall in 1592, then after being ordained, began working among the poor of London in 1619. During the terrible years of the plague he administered to the sick and dying, but in spite of his good work he was arrested and condemned to death in 1654.

After John Southworth was executed, the Spanish Ambassador secretly paid for his body to be sewn together and embalmed, then taken abroad to the English College at Douai where he had been trained. The local people then began to pray at his shrine, with several miraculous cures being attributed to his intercession. In 1789, due to the turmoil of the French Revolution, his body was buried for safety and its location forgotten. But in 1926, at a time when his beatification was being promoted, by chance it was rediscovered by workmen digging the foundations of a shop. After it was positively identified, it was returned once more to England to become one of the church's most prized relics.

Chapter Six

A Hidden Past

Lancelot's Shire

There are romantics who question the widely accepted view that the name of Lancashire is derived from Lon Castrum, which was the Roman fort on the banks of the River Lune. In their view Lancashire was originally Lancelot's Shire, having taken its name from the noble Sir Lancelot who ruled over part of the North West. There are also numerous other traditions which, they point out, link the elusive King Arthur and his knights of the Round Table with the Red Rose county. Sceptics are, of course, scornful of such claims, some believing that most of Arthur's adventures never took place, being just fanciful fiction.

True, it is difficult to separate myth from reality when looking at the exploits of one of Britain's heroes, for since the 12th century writers and artists and poets have created their own Arthurian vision. Before this much of what we know of Arthur was passed down orally from one generation to the next, but this also had its mixture of fact and fantasy.

So what we are left with today is a rich tapestry woven from both truth and legend. At times his exploits sweep us away into a magical land of romance and adventure which could be part of a child's bedtime story, then quite suddenly we are brought down to earth by known historical facts. Later, perhaps, we become even more puzzled when we discover that what we have taken to be merely fascinating legends have hidden meanings. For behind what appear to be entertaining tales of adventure lie deeper questions of human morality which are significant to every age.

So who was King Arthur? It is believed that he was not really a king but a great Celtic warrior who lived during the fifth or sixth century. This was the period of the Dark Ages when the Romans, after four centuries, had left Britain. The country was still in transition, with newly formed kingdoms fighting both among themselves and against the Anglo-Saxon invaders.

Arthur's birthplace is open to speculation, being claimed by Cornwall, Wales and Northern England. His father was Uther Pendragon, who may have lived in Cumbria, and his mother was Igrain who came from Cornwall. It is said that due to his outstanding fighting prowess he was able to bring together several Celtic kings, becoming the head of their multi-tribal army. From their ranks he probably drew his cavalry 'officers' which formed what is now known as the familiar Knights of the Round Table. Their task was to oppose the Anglo-Saxons, which they did magnificently. The invaders were contained, leading eventually to a peaceful compromise, with Arthur and his knights becoming the great heroes of their day.

It is said that Arthur fought twelve decisive battles, some of which, according to local tradition, took place in Lancashire. The banks of the River Douglas, a narrow waterway which begins on Rivington Moor then winds a gentle path around Wigan to join the Ribble beyond Tarleton, is said to be one of these sites. A legend links Scholes Bank in Horwich to one battle, while others are said to have taken place at Blackrod and Wigan. Bamber Bridge is where some believe he fought his last battle, being mortally wounded by Mordred, his incestuously begotten son.

Parbold, Burscough, Sefton and Birkdale all claim Arthurian connections, while his principal knight, Sir Lancelot of the Lake, is forever associated with Martin Mere. The son of King Ban, Lancelot had an adulterous affair with Guinevere and was banished from court. His own child grew up to become the chivalrous Sir Galahad who was one of the three successful Grail Knights. After Arthur's death, Lancelot ended his days as a hermit.

The first written mention of Arthur dates from the 7th century, in a document concerning the life of Saint Columba, then his name occurs later in Welsh verse. But it was a 12th-century historian, Geoffrey of Monmouth, who brought Arthur to prominence in his book *A History of the Kings of Britain*. Written in Latin, this work relates tales which had been told for five centuries around the firesides of England. Fact became mingled with colourful fiction, Arthur became a king and his warriors of the 5th century were transformed into Norman knights.

Over the next six centuries many other writers followed the lead given by Geoffrey of Monmouth, each adding their own interpretations of Arthur's world. This celebration of Arthur and his world of Celtic magic continues today; full of symbolism and philosophy it has a timeless appeal. Added to this for the Lancastrian is the intriguing possibility that many of his greatest adventures took place in our corner of England.

Radcliffe's Fair Ellen

Radcliffe is an ancient town with roots deep in Saxon England. Washed by two rivers, the Irwell and the Roch, it was once held by Edward the Confessor. Soon after the Norman invasion the manor was administered by the Radcliffes who later held the office of High Sheriff. Their home, Radcliffe Tower, is now a sad ruin but once it was among Lancashire's finest buildings. Originally erected as a thick-walled pele to repel the Scots, it was rebuilt during the early 15th century, enjoying an enviable position in a green valley. Not until the early 19th century did it fall into disrepair when part of it was used as a cowshed. However, today it is largely remembered not for its former beauty, but for a horrific murder; a terrible event which tore the Radcliffe family apart and became the subject of the enduring ballad *Fair Ellen of Radcliffe*.

The tragedy began when following the birth of a daughter to the Lord of the Manor, his wife died. The child, named Ellen, grew up to be a great beauty who was adored by her doting father. However, when he re-married his new wife became possessed with concealed jealousy of her stepdaughter. This envy became worse over the years, until when Ellen reached eighteen and her beauty was at its height, her stepmother could stand it no longer. Consumed with hatred she came up with an evil plot to dispose of Ellen forever.

It was while the Lord and his fellow aristocrats were enjoying a day out hunting deer in his vast Radcliffe estate, that the stepmother began to execute the plan. The ladies had gathered on a vantage point to watch the chase, then when it was about to end the stepmother asked Ellen if she would return to the Tower to tell the master cook to prepare the evening meal. "He must kill the milk-white doe from the park and bake it in a pie," she was told.

In the kitchen Ellen found the master cook, together with the scullion boy. She gave the apparently innocent message, but unknown to her it had a far more sinister meaning. Immediately the cook picked up his sharp knife and walked towards her. The horrified scullion boy, anticipating what was about to happen, helplessly pleaded for her life, offering his own instead. But the evil man was set on his terrible task, threatening to kill the boy as

The remains of ancient Radcliffe Tower

well if he revealed the deed. In the space of a few seconds Ellen was brutally murdered.

When the laughing hunting party returned to the Tower the meal was set before them, the large milk-white doe pie being placed on the table. The lord was puzzled that his devoted daughter was not present as it was the custom for her to sit by his side. He asked his jealous wife to call Ellen, but was astonished to learn that, "She has fled from home to live in a nunnery. You must forget her. Let our guests eat."

Full of disbelief he stood up before his friends, vowing that he would never again eat or drink until he saw his daughter. At that instant the scullion boy ran into the room. Pointing to the pie, he quickly related the horrific tale of murder, telling how the body of the beautiful Ellen, which had been minced into tiny pieces, now lay on the table ready to be eaten.

While the guests looked on in hushed silence, the lord, overcome with a mixture of grief and anger, immediately pronounced judgement on his cruel wife and her accomplice. She suffered death by being burnt at the stake, while the evil master cook was boiled in oil. The scullion boy, who had done so much to try to prevent the tragedy, was made heir to the estate, which he eventually inherited.

For centuries this sad story which ended in apparent justice was told and retold throughout the county. It is said that many people made pilgrimages to Radcliffe church to see the effigy of both Ellen and her father. Sometimes they would break pieces off the grave slab, believing that these acted as charms against sickness.

Mysterious Longridge

Overlooking the winding path of the River Ribble to the north of Ribchester and Hurst Green, Longridge Fell dominates the skyline. From Kemple End, which lies at its eastern edge, wooded slopes rise steeply upwards from the banks of the Hodder, ending in a sea of windswept heather and moorland grass. During the Civil War Cromwell marched his troops along this lonely moor before scattering the Royalists at the battle of Preston. Its wildness later fuelled the imagination of the young Conan Doyle who was a pupil at nearby Stonyhurst College.

It is not surprising that this unspoilt and ancient landscape boasts a host of both historic associations and strange legends. These may at first seem highly fanciful, perhaps being dismissed by many as fiction from a colourful past. However, what cannot be ignored is the evidence that remains which gives puzzling credibility to the tales.

Rising upwards to the south-west of the fell is a farm track with the curious name of Written Stone Lane. It is a former Roman road which linked the fort at Ribchester to Lancaster. Partly hidden by overhanging foliage on the side of the track is a huge slab of stone which has an intriguing message neatly carved on its edge:

Ravffe Radcliffe Laid This
Stone To Lye For Ever: AD1655

There are several strange tales associated with the Written Stone which go only part-way to explain the odd inscription. One of these tells how a murder was committed in the area which led to the victim's ghost haunting the site seeking retribution. It seems that the Radcliffe family, who were local landowners, were connected with the affair and suffered most from the malevolent spirit. Several unexpected deaths attributed to the haunting occurred in the family, which caused them a great deal of distress.

Ralph Radcliffe, who was the head of the family, decided that action must be taken. He called in a local priest who carried out an exorcism by praying in the haunted lane and the nearby farm. After this service the carved stone was placed in position, acting as a declaration of the event. It seemed to have worked at the time for the Radcliffes were afterwards left in peace.

However, the ghost did not permanently leave the secluded lane for odd scratching sounds and unexplained screeches have been heard by later travellers, who became reluctant to pass that way at night. A local doctor saw a dark form materialise close to the stone. This quickly began to spread, enveloping both himself and his horse. He then experienced a horrible choking sensation, later believing himself lucky to have escaped from the terrifying ordeal alive.

It may well be that the origins of the Written Stone go much further back in time than these stories suggest. The large slab is of such an unusual size that it may well have once acted as a pagan altar, perhaps even having been used for human sacrifice, giving rise to its sinister reputation.

Another strange tale related about the Longridge area concerns a miraculous cow. Perched above the doorway of a cottage which lies down an ancient lane, can still be seen what is said to be the remains of one of its ribs. The rest of the animal was buried at nearby Grimsargh, the spot being identified on the Ordnance Survey map as Cow Hill.

It is said that several centuries ago the district was suffering from a severe drought that threatened the livelihood of the local people. At first the unbroken sunshine was welcomed, but as the weeks wore on without any rain the farmers began to get worried. Reading the country signs, including seeing bats flying during the daytime, they knew that it was likely to continue for months. The ground became rock-hard, the grass withered, streams and wells dried up. Farm animals could not be fed so many had to be reluctantly killed.

It was when the drought was at its height that the miracle occurred. As the villagers gazed up to the fell, hoping for a sign of clouds, they noticed a movement on the hillside. A closer inspection revealed a huge, dun-

A rib from the miraculous cow preserved at Longridge

coloured cow, which surprisingly looked in remarkable health. The animal was taken to the village where it was milked, and it continued to give an unending supply of the precious liquid for weeks. Never running dry, it saved hundreds from starvation, until at last the drought came to a dramatic end.

However, the tale of the miraculous cow had reached the ears of an old woman from Pendle who had a reputation for dealing in the occult. She arrived at Longridge to test the beast; sitting on a stool she began milking the animal, passing the milk through a sieve. She continued for over a day, filling all manner of receptacles, but when night came the poor animal fell to the ground exhausted, then died. It had saved the village but had been killed by the woman's greed.

Another local tradition concerns the terrifying apparition of a headless woman. From behind she is said to look normal, her tightly fitting clothes and coal-scuttle bonnet hiding her grim secret. Any stranger who tries to speak to her might assume it is shyness that makes her face away, but as she turns they will see an empty bonnet. As they gaze in horror, she removes the top from her basket to reveal her decapitated head. This then gives a horrifying laugh before flying through the air, its jaws viciously snapping, to chase the innocent victim.

One evening a local man was returning from a drinking session at an isolated inn, his homeward path lying across the lonely fellside. He was unfortunate in meeting the headless woman, her detached head beginning the inevitable chase. Luckily he was a healthy man who was used to climbing the steep hills, so he was able to outrun the pursuing head, reaching the safety of his cottage. However, he received little sympathy from his wife when she heard the tale, "if it makes you glad of your own hearthside I'll be more than pleased, for its more than a woman with a head on her shoulders can do!"

Screaming Skulls

As well as the relics of saints which are kept in several Lancashire churches for religious purposes, other human remains have been retained more as curiosities. Most of these are skulls, which are probably a link with our Celtic ancestors for they regarded the human head as a powerful magical symbol. They believed that the head remained alive after the body had died, and a severed head was a charm against evil. Sculptured heads in different materials became an important part of their culture, some of their gods being shown with three heads.

The Appley Bridge skull

One of these human relics is to be found in Affetside, a fascinating hilltop village which straggles a former Roman road to the north of Bury. According to local tradition, the ancient village cross, which stands on the roadside, marks the exact mid-point between London and Edinburgh, and the community boasts that it was one of Lancashire's last villages to receive piped drinking water; which finally arrived in 1972. At its centre stands the Pack Horse pub, which was named after the strings of packhorses which once carried cotton goods over this lonely ridge. Today it is a popular haven, but many a visitor has been startled when ordering his first pint, for looking out from above the cosy bar is a mahogany-coloured human skull.

The skull which now decorates the hostelry is that of George Whowell, a farmer who lived in the area during the period of the Civil War. It is said that one day he returned to his isolated moorland home on the edge of Turton Moor to find that a band of Royalist soldiers had massacred his wife and children. Absolutely distraught at the sight, he made a vow that one day he would avenge the callous murders.

His opportunity came a few years later following the Battle of Worcester when the future King Charles II barely escaped with his life. The Earl of Derby, the leader of Lancashire's Royalists, was captured by Cromwell's soldiers, then sent to Chester. After a short trial he was sentenced to death, which because of his status as an aristocrat was to be by beheading. As Bolton people had greatly suffered at the hands of the Royalists, with 1200 citizens having been slaughtered, it was considered appropriate that the Earl's execution should take place in the town.

Surprisingly, in view of the atrocities, many onlookers wept openly as the earl was taken on his final journey through the streets on that fateful day in 1651. His final hour was spent in the Man and Scythe Inn in Churchgate. He then climbed up to the scaffold which had been built from wood from his home, Lathom House. But George Whowell had no thoughts of mercy; the anguished faces of his murdered family were forever etched on his mind. It seemed that justice had prevailed when he offered his services as the executioner, then beheaded the tragic earl in front of a large crowd.

The earl's body was put in a short coffin and his severed head in a separate casket, then placed in the family vault in Ormskirk church. But how George Whowell's skull ended up in the bar of the Pack Horse is unrecorded. It is likely that following his death, and the jubilation of the Restoration, the new regime sought revenge. Perhaps placing the skull in the inn to ridicule him.

Another mystery surrounds the whereabouts of the executioner's axe and block, which for a century were held by the Whowell family of Edgworth. They passed to the Holt family of Turton, then were sold to William Sharples of the Star Inn Museum in Bolton who retained them for some years. The last known owner is believed to have been James P. Weston during the last century, since when it seems to have disappeared.

At Appley Bridge near Wigan is kept another human skull which has given its name to Skull House. This 400-year-old private home is mysterious in character, being full of odd corners, boarded-up cellars and suspected priest's hiding holes. Its leaded windows are decorated with skulls, signifying that it is the resting place of a large human skull which is known affectionately as Charlie. Highly polished, it is kept in a special box in the living room, its true identity being in dispute.

One tale links it to a great battle which is said to have been fought by King Arthur and his knights on the banks of the Douglas which flows close by.

Centuries later the skull of a slaughtered knight was unearthed, then placed in the house for safe keeping. Another legend suggests that Charlie was a monk who lived in the 17th century, and was decapitated by Cromwell's soldiers. A forensic report says, however, that the skull belonged to a woman, which contradicts the previous tales, so perhaps Charlie should really be Charlotte. The skull is now treated with great respect for it is considered bad luck to even move it. One former owner decided to toss it back into the river, but mysteriously it appeared back in the house!

Lying in the heart of the Ribble Valley, close to the hamlet of Bashall Eaves, ancient Browsholme Hall is popular with visitors who come to explore this attractive area. The present house was built by Edmund Parker in 1507 to replace an older, timber and daub building which had been erected in the 14th century. The Parker family name was derived from the office of park keeper, with succeeding generations holding distinguished positions within Lancashire, including that of High Sheriff and Deputy Lieutenant.

Visitors to the house see a host of fascinating objects which have been acquired by the family over many centuries, but perhaps the most interesting item is seldom put on public view. The Browsholme Skull is kept hidden securely away in a cupboard in the Tudor Hall; the family, being well aware of its past history, treat it with the greatest respect. It is thought to have belonged to a martyr who died during the Pilgrimage of Grace, fighting against the closure of the monasteries. Originally the relic was kept in the chapel, then in 1703 it was moved to its present position when the house was extended.

But it was in the middle of the last century when young Edmund Parker, a student at Harrow School, decided to play a practical joke that disaster struck. When he secretly took the skull then buried it in the garden, a series of terrible events hit the household. The façade of the building began to fall away from the walls, a number of unexplained fires broke out in the ancient beams, then death after death struck the family.

In frightened desperation the youth confessed to his escapade, the skull was retrieved and reverently returned to the cupboard. Happily, events at Browsholme slowly returned to normality, but the family had to move out for two years while the house was fully repaired. So this distressing episode in the history of the family is always impressed upon the younger members, it being emphasised that the skull must not be moved!

Turton Tower is another of Lancashire's fine ancient buildings, having been first erected during the 12th century as a sturdy refuge from the raiding Scots. It lies on the edge of rising moorland near the village of Edgworth, attracting visitors to its impressive rooms and fascinating museum of local objects. One display attracts a great deal of attention for it houses the famous Timberbottom skulls and Bible.

About the year 1750, a farmer was working on his land near Bradshaw Brook, which is situated to the north of Bolton. He noticed something glinting in the water so waded out and retrieved two objects which he found to be human skulls. These he took home to Timberbottom Farm, where he placed them on the mantelpiece as rather grisly relics.

Shortly after this event strange and frightening noises were heard around the farm, crockery rattled in the kitchen, animals became petrified with fear, and loud footsteps were heard ascending the staircase. When the farmer began to investigate he found a terrifying scene in an upstairs room. The ghostly figure of two men were engaged in a ferocious fight, watched by the spectral figure of a girl.

The household learned to live with the ghostly happenings for many years, then in 1840 it was decided to give the skulls a decent burial in Bradshaw churchyard, which it was hoped would rid the farm of the spirits. Unfortunately, this was unsuccessful, the hauntings continued so the skulls were once more retrieved and this time placed on a family Bible within Bradshaw Hall.

This new home proved effective, bringing tranquillity to Timberbottom Farm, but it was found that if the skulls were separated the hauntings returned. When Bradshaw Hall was due to be demolished the skulls and bible were taken to Turton Tower for safe keeping, where they remain.

One explanation of the hauntings tells how a young man who worked at the farm as a servant fell in love with a daughter of the wealthy Bradshaw family of Bradshaw Hall. Her brother, appalled at the audacity of the would-be suitor, attacked and killed him. For many years the girl wandered forlornly around the district looking for her lover, not knowing the truth. Only in death did they find true happiness, both their skulls and their spirits being brought together.

Another version relates how in the 17th century a manservant was left in charge of the farm. A band of three mounted robbers appeared during the night, then attempted to enter the building through the small window of the Cheese Room. The servant having heard them arrive, waited with his sword at the ready and in the resulting fight two of the robbers were decapitated. The remaining thief, in an attempt to hide the identity of his companions, escaped with their two heads, later tossing them into the Bradshaw Brook.

Little People

The supernatural world of fairies is now almost completely restricted to children's story books, any possibility that such creatures ever existed being scoffed at by most adults. Yet our northern ancestors had no such doubts for a belief in the existence of the little people was a living legacy from prehistoric times. This belief was, of course, not restricted to England for in many corners of the world similar tales are told. Often these little people were said to have human bodies, but with features such as pointed ears or wings, and most possessed supernatural powers. Generally, they were considered to be neither gods nor ghosts, but merely a race apart.

A belief in fairies was common throughout Lancashire, having been greatly influenced by the Celtic tradition. The name 'fairy' is a general term for several different races of the little people. 'Elf' was originally the Anglo-Saxon equivalent of fairy, but later became the term used only for a very small fairy. 'Brownies' lived in domestic surroundings, while 'goblins', commonly known in Lancashire as 'boggarts', were grotesque, mischievous and sometimes even evil. 'Hobgoblins' were generally considered to be friendly and helpful, 'gnomes' were associated with the earth, while 'pixies', which were uncommon in Lancashire, were said to be the spirits of children who had died unbaptised.

One traditional tale relates that in Penwortham Woods, not far from the banks of the Ribble, a fairy funeral is sometimes seen. Anyone who is unlucky enough to view the strange spectacle should beware for it is an omen of imminent death. Two farmworkers were returning home at midnight when, by chance, they came upon the cortège winding its way along a path that led from the ancient churchyard. In amazement one of the men gazed down at the miniature coffin, then to his horror he saw that the face of the corpse was his own. Within a month the man was dead, having fallen from a haystack. Ironically his funeral passed along the same route taken by the fairy funeral.

Now a green oasis on the outskirts of Manchester, Boggart Hole Clough derived its name from a mischievous fairy which lives in the area. It is said that his shrieks of laughter can still be heard echoing through the woods in springtime. But in spite of all the signs of his presence he has never actually been seen by human eye, always managing to keep one step ahead.

One particularly cold winter the boggart decided to forsake the woodland, seeking refuge in the house of a farmer named George Cheetham who lived nearby. Soon the household was thrown into complete chaos by his tricks, with kitchen tools being hidden, the children's food being snatched from their hands and bowls being tossed across the room. One child found the boggart's lair behind woodwork at the foot of the stairs, for items that were put through a small hole in the wall were flung back with fury. The boggart's presence cast despair over the farm. The farmer's two sons were harassed every night as they slept, eerie laughter filled the bedroom, powerful hands gripped their bodies and they were tossed around the room. Distressed by the whole episode, the farmer finally decided that the family must leave the building.

Packing all the household furniture onto a number of carts, the family set off to their new home. Passing through the village they stopped to tell a neighbour the reason for their departure and a voice shouted from one of the milk churns on their cart, "Aye, Aye, neighbour we're flittin a'reet as tha sees." The amazed farmer turned to his family, realizing that the boggart was still with them, he said it was pointless them moving home so they returned to their old farm. Thankfully, after this episode the boggart calmed down, his exploits became less serious and the family learned to accept his presence.

One boggart that is particularly unwelcome is the shriker, for when this appears it is said that death is not far away. It sometimes takes the form of an animal, usually a white horse, a cow or a dog. It is recorded that a shriker in the form of a headless dog attacked a man near Manchester's old church in 1825, chasing him all the way home.

In picturesque Garstang lives the Boggart of the Brook, which is associated with the spirit of a murdered woman. She would beg a lift from any passing horseman, then when mounted behind him would unwrap her cloak and hood to reveal she was a skeleton. The shock of feeling her bony fingers would cause such terror that the horseman would fall and inevitably die.

At Oldham it was Chamber Hall that was troubled by a boggart, the household being brought to a standstill by its outrageous antics, while at Rochdale goblins are said to have been responsible for moving the building materials when St Chad's church was first being erected.

Raising the Dead

One moonlit autumn night in the late 16th century, two men crept furtively into St Leonard's churchyard at Walton-le-dale, near Preston. One was Edward Kelley, an unscrupulous practitioner of magic and astrology. Some years previously he had had his ears removed at Lancaster Castle as punishment for his crimes so to hide his disfigurement he wore a tight-fitting, black cap. Guiding him through the maze of gravestones was Paul Waring, a local man from Clayton Brook who was familiar with the ancient churchyard. It was essential that their extraordinary mission should not be discovered for they were about to experiment with the forbidden art of necromancy, raising the dead to discover their secrets.

In the darkness Waring pointed out to his companion the site of a newly dug grave which contained the remains of a rich man. He had died without revealing the location of a fortune he was known to possess so the task was to obtain the dead man's secret. Quickly the coffin was unearthed, then the lid was ripped off to reveal the rotting corpse. Kelley then began to perform his ritual magic, chanting his weird words and waving a wand above the body until it started to flicker into life. According to tradition, not only did the dead man tell where his money lay hidden, but he also made a number of predictions concerning the lives of local people, all of which proved to be true!

Kelley's path into the occult had begun when he became associated with Dr John Dee, one of the most famous astrologers of the time. Dee, a member of a wealthy Welsh family had been born in London in 1527. He attended St

John's College at Cambridge, then after a period abroad he returned to become a Fellow of the newly created Trinity College. He became a distinguished mathematician with an international reputation, but his leanings towards experiments in astrology and magic made him a controversial character.

In 1547 King Edward received him at court, awarding him a pension, and for a period he went to live at Upton-on-Severn. However, his reputation for carrying out occult practices continued to cause concern, leading to him being accused of casting spells on Queen Mary. He spent time in prison before being acquitted, then following the accession of Elizabeth found himself once more in favour. Using his knowledge of astrology he was asked to decide on the most favourable date for her coronation in 1558.

His pursuit of science continued during the following years, knowing few boundaries. He interwove mathematics and magic, superstition and astrology, venturing into the quest for an elixir of life. Edward Kelley, an Oxford scholar, now became his constant companion, aiding him with his controversial experiments. But many members of the public were outraged by the tales of occult practices which were said to take place at his house in Surrey. In 1583 an enraged mob attacked his home, destroying his library of 4000 priceless books and manuscripts.

Both Dee and Kelley fled the country for Bohemia, where they teamed up with Albert Laski, a learned Polish aristocrat. They had many adventures as they travelled through Europe, exploiting the public's taste for magical beliefs. Kelley was at first very popular abroad, being knighted by the Germans as a tribute to his conjuring powers. But Dee, who himself had few moral principles, eventually found Kelley's ability to venture into the 'worst kinds of magic' too much: the friendship came to an end. Kelley's reputation than began to plunge, public opinion turned against him and he landed up in jail. His death followed in 1595 from injuries sustained while making a bid for freedom.

In 1596, after Dee returned to England, he again found fame when Elizabeth rewarded him with the post of Warden of Manchester College. This he held for seven years and he became a friend of many of Lancashire's gentry, who often sought his advice. His initial celebrity status began to flounder as many began to question his philosophy. Eventually, on the death of Elizabeth in 1603, he was forced to flee back to London, where he died five years later in poverty.

Eagle and Child

In many parts of Lancashire there are pub signs which show the eagle and child, which is the crest of the powerful Stanley family. This is a reminder of a strange event which took place 600 years ago during the reign of

Edward III. At that time both Sir Thomas, who was head of the family who lived at Lathom Hall, and his devoted wife Isabel, were advancing in years, but had no son to inherit their estate. In desperation Sir Thomas took a mistress named Mary Oskatell, who eventually gave birth to a baby boy which he had desired so much. However, his next problem lay in how he could introduce the child into his household, making it acceptable to his wife.

After much soul-searching he devised a plan which involved the baby being placed by his servant beneath a tree on his estate in which an eagle was nesting. He then told Isabel that he had come upon the child by chance, that the bird had probably carried it to the spot in its talons. This miraculous happening was a gift from heaven he told her, for they now had a son they could cherish.

The child, who was baptised Oskatell, was quickly accepted into the family and later became the heir to the title and estate. To perpetuate the supposed miracle, Sir Thomas made an eagle his crest, showing it with outspread wings and its head turning as if looking for the baby which it had lost. However, in spite of his elaborate plan Sir Thomas probably knew that his wife had never really been taken in by the hoax. In old age he finally confessed to her that Sir Oskatell was only his illegitimate son, his true heir being her descendants. After his death they changed the family crest to the eagle and child to emphasise that Sir Oskatell had no claim on the estate.

At Standishgate in Wigan the remains of Mab's Cross is a reminder of another colourful marital episode from the past which occurred during the reign of Edward I. It involved Sir William Bradshaw of Haigh Hall and his wife Mabel, who as a member of the rich Norris family had brought a large inheritance to their marriage. It is believed that Sir William became involved in a local rebellion against the powerful Earl of Lancaster, known as the Banastre Rising. It proved unsuccessful so Sir William was forced to flee abroad to escape his enemies, leaving his wife in charge of the estate.

After he had been absent from Haigh for over seven years Lady Mabel was forced to conclude that living in such a lawless time he had probably been killed. She was finding running the estate single- handed a great burden so finally she accepted the advances of a Welsh knight, whom she married. However, this proved to be a disastrous relationship, her new husband took complete control of her wealth, treating her badly.

Three years later, while she was distributing her customary charity to the poor, she suddenly recognised the face of a beggar in the crowd – it was Sir William who had returned. Having learned from his tenants the distress that the Welsh knight had caused, he was determined to seek retribution. Hearing of Sir William's return, however, the knight fled towards his homeland, with Sir William in grim pursuit. Eventually the Welshman was overtaken near Newton-le-Willows, and a fierce fight followed ending in his death.

At last Lady Mabel was happily reunited with her husband, but the distress of having been a party to a bigamous marriage still hung over her. As a penance her confessor ordered her to walk 'onest every week bare-foute and bare-legged to a cross nere Wigan called Mabb Cross'. In Wigan parish church the splendid Bradshaw tomb marks the last resting place of the couple. They had no children so their fortune was split between her cousin, Alan Norris, and Sir William's brother, John Bradshaw. In later centuries the family fortune became even greater for their land around Wigan was found to be rich in coal. Today Haigh Hall and its grounds, which are owned by Wigan Corporation, are open to the public.

The Eagle and Child

Odd Legends

On the 8th October 1629 a magistrate heard a strange tale told by Christopher Baron, a husbandman. He stated in evidence that James Brewer of Penwortham near Preston had some twenty years earlier possessed a stone which was red-coloured on one side and black-coloured on the other, and when raked with a pin would bleed. He had obtained the stone from a spirit. Baron had heard the tale from William Proctor, and two other people confirmed it, having heard Brewer and Baron in discussion. The magistrate noted the claims, but apparently the stone was never produced so the case was not pursued.

Towering above the impressive moorland valley of Cliviger Gorge, near Burnley stands Eagle Crag, a lonely spot which has long been associated with witchcraft and hauntings. According to a local tradition it is here on this windswept moorland that Lady Sybil, a practitioner of the black art and wife of Lord William Towneley, lies buried.

It was widely known that the beautiful Sybil was a witch, yet in spite of this Lord William fell deeply in love with her. It is reputed that she could change her form at will, becoming a cat or a white doe, then she would roam as she pleased over the empty moorlands. Initially she had not responded to the advances of the young aristocrat, but he called for help from another local witch to give him the power to attract her. He was told to go to Eagle Crag on All Saint's Day and to hunt for the white doe. With the aid of a magical dog he managed to trap the animal, then he secured it with an enchanted silken rope. The doe immediately changed into the form of Sybil, who agreed to stop her life of sorcery and become Lord William's wife.

However, their married life together was short for Sybil could not resist returning to her wanton ways. She caused all manner of trouble in the district, including damaging machinery at a local mill while disguised as a cat. This led to her having a hand cut off by the machinery, then ended with her death. Her body was buried beneath the crag, but each Hallowe'en she returns as a ghostly white doe which can be seen being chased across the moors by hounds and huntsmen.

On another moorland high point above Bacup there once stood a pool of brown, peaty water, which is reputed to have been a favourite washing place for the devil. It was an isolated place, hidden by mounds of purple heather, being known only to a few shepherds. When they heard the sound of splashing coming from the pool, they knew Owd Nick had come down to bathe.

One bitterly cold winter night Owd Nick came to the pool, hoping to gain shelter from the wind behind a large boulder that stood nearby. But when he reached the spot he was dismayed to find that the torrential rain had filled the hollow which contained the pool, causing it to overflow. The rapid movement of the water had created a huge channel which looked as if it might completely drain his favourite pool.

Speeding through the air towards a pile of rocks which lay on the moorland edge, he picked them up and tried to dam the torrent. But the water pressure was too great, it immediately swept them away. Looking around for something more substantial, he grabbed a tarpaulin from a haystack, then filled it with huge stones. However, this proved not to be strong enough, the sheet broke, and the stones were scattered across the moorland. The rain continued for many hours, expanding the channel until the pool completely drained away. This is now known as Hell Clough, and the stones Owd Nick dropped can still be seen scattered in the valley.

Werneth Low Country Park which lies on the fringe of Manchester has associations not with Owd Nick, but with that legendary outlaw of Sherwood Forest, Robin Hood. It is said that he and his men came here to have a competition of skill and endurance. To prove his superiority Robin tossed a huge rock in the direction of Cheshire. It landed in the River Tame at Hulmes Wood where it still remains, and his hand print can be seen on its surface.

Chapter Seven

Colourful Customs

A Legacy from the Past

In Lancashire we celebrate many strange and colourful rituals that create a marvellous atmosphere of laughter and gaiety. Pace-egging at Easter, bonfires, morris dancing and rush-bearing services are just a few of these many customs which are carried out with great enthusiasm. Today they are largely treated light-heartedly, with few of us questioning the origins of these events. Yet in many cases what has now evolved into a carnival celebration was begun by our ancestors as a deadly serious pagan ceremony.

A young egg roller at Avenham Park, Preston

Although many of our northern customs probably had their origins in the religious beliefs of the Stone Age, it was the highly imaginative Celts who brought these to new heights. Each Celtic tribe was ruled over by a High-King, followed in social order by lesser-kings, nobles, chiefs, freemen and bondsmen. But much of the real power lay with the highly academic druids who had their own system of hierarchy, having magicians, astrologers and religious poets among their ranks. It is from their teachings that many of our customs have evolved.

Their elaborate religious ceremonies seem to have revolved around the wonder of nature. These were often carried out in a forest grove, being a form of tree-worship. They venerated the oak, together with the mistletoe which sometimes grew upon its branches. This was cut down by a druid using a Golden Sickle, then distributed to the worshippers. The mistletoe is regarded by some historians as being the celebrated Golden Bough.

Druidic festivals took place four times a year, dates which are still remembered in our calendar. Oimelc is now Candlemas, Beltane is May Day, Samhain is All Saint's Day and Lagnasad is August Bank Holiday. Another festival took place around what is now Christmas Day, while the passing of the seasons was related to the ages of man. Many of these mysterious rituals, often modified over the centuries, have become absorbed into our Christian culture, while others have survived to form part of our village customs. In some cases what began as an elaborate and solemn ceremony of the Celts, now merely brings a touch of colour to our village greens in May.

Closely associated with the religious beliefs of the ancient world are superstitions, which although we may be reluctant to admit it, still form part of many of our lives. These have evolved from an in-born desire to explain our very existence, to avoid misfortune, and in the case of omens to look into an uncertain future.

Pace-Egging

Chocolate Easter eggs, which for many weeks prior to Easter are piled high on our supermarket shelves, are the latest version of the painted and decorated eggs which were part of the early pagan celebrations. Later they became known as Pace eggs, taking their name from Pasch, which is the Jewish Passover and the Christian Easter festival. These hard-boiled eggs are still rolled down the hillside by children at Avenham Park in Preston and at West Derby in Liverpool on Easter Monday, symbolically 'rolling away the stone'.

Lancashire's traditional pace-eggers are men. They perpetuate one of our most colourful village customs which has evolved into a light-hearted celebration of Easter. They once dressed in eccentric clothes, sometimes wearing jackets inside out or caps back to front, with blackened faces and false beards. Parading through their home village or town, they entered the houses begging for pace-eggs, food or money. Inevitably their path eventually led to the village inn, where thirst was quenched and the horseplay became more boisterous. Part of the fun lay in their disguise as they attempted to pass unrecognised among their friends.

The custom, which stretches back many centuries, had its local variations. In Blackburn the pace-eggers, who wore animal skins, were led by Old Toss Pot who carried the Easter eggs. Music, singing and dancing prevailed, with a colourful carnival atmosphere following the group through the town. However, at times this changed to rowdiness, with fighting breaking out. It is recorded that about 1843 'a gang of fellows styled the Carr-laners (who lived in Carr Lane, Blackburn) armed with bludgeons, endeavoured to despoil the pace-eggers. Numerous fights, with the usual concomitants of broken eggs and various contusions, were amongst the results.'

Pace-egg plays, also known as mumming plays in parts of Lancashire, became a feature of the custom. In ritualistic fashion, the disguised players would wander through their village acting out a fight between good and evil. Saint George would meet his adversary, Slasher the Turkish Knight, which would lead to a mock sword fight. The winner, of course, was St George, who would kill his enemy, but then a doctor would bring the dead man back to life. A figure wearing a horse's head in some cases formed part of the cast, with a traditional pace-egging song being sung.

Pace-egging continued into the early years of this century then began to decline. However, the 1960s brought a welcome revival of interest in folk drama of all kinds, and now a number of pace-eggers, including those at Bury and Middleton, are continuing the tradition at Eastertime. The Bury team start their annual performance on the Saturday before Good Friday, at noon in the square in the town. They continue their tour of the local villages through the following week, while the Middleton group perform their colourful rituals on Easter Monday.

Morris Dancers and Mummers

Perhaps nothing typifies Lancashire in springtime more than the sight of a troop of morris men carrying out their elaborate routines on a village green. With flower-bedecked hats, tinkling bells and shining clogs, these folk dancers bring with them a welcome splash of colour together with a link to the past. But morris dancing is not solely English, for similar traditions occur in many parts of Europe. The term 'morris', although now almost always associated with dancing, originally referred to a rich variety of folk routines. It is believed that this, too, has its origins in prehistoric times, being part of pagan ceremonies. Some sword dances terminate with mock executions, which suggest they might once have been associated with ritual human sacrifice.

During the 16th century the dances became very popular, spreading to other parts of the world where the British settled. After the Civil War the Puritans temporarily ended much of this merriment, the dances being localised, surviving mainly in isolated rural areas. Generally they were associated with May Day and Whitsuntide celebrations, but in Lancashire they were also part of the rush bearing ceremonies and wakes week.

The last half century has witnessed a welcome revival of these customs, with Lancashire now boasting many morris and sword and clog teams who carry out a hectic programme throughout the summer. As well as regular an-

Two of Bacup's famous Coconut Dancers at Clitheroe

nual displays, they perform at fairs, accompany parades and attend folk festivals. Some of these take place abroad, leading to an exchange of ideas on the distribution and origins of their dances.

Bacup's Britannia Coconut Dancers, with their blackened faces and highly polished clogs, are one of Lancashire's most colourful teams. It is believed that their unique routine evolved from dances which were first brought to England by Moorish pirates during the 17th century. Having made their home in Cornwall, their descendants worked in the tin mines, then later moved north to Lancashire, finding employment in the quarries and mines around Bacup. They brought with them these traditional dances, many of which celebrate the coming of spring.

Known affectionately as the Nutters, the dancers dress in red and white kilts, black jerseys, white stockings and wear very decorative, turban-like hats. For their spring ritual dance they carry half-hoop garlands decorated with red, white and blue flowers and are accompanied by music from an English concertina. Their unique Coconut Dance involves each dancer tapping out rhythms on wooden discs known as nuts which are attached to their hands, waist and knees.

Formed in 1857, they remain the only surviving troupe of five which originally performed in the Rossendale district. Their main event takes place every Easter Saturday when, accompanied by Stacksteads Brass Band, they dance from boundary to boundary across Bacup. Stopping at every public house on the route, each publican rewards the dancers with a free drink, which ensures a rousing end to the day!

In the windswept Lancashire villages which lie high on the Pennines close to the Yorkshire border, in wintertime the morris men were replaced by mummers or sweepers. Traditionally, it was New Year's Eve when groups of both men and women would 'sweep' through cottages and farms with a broom.

Often the sexes would change clothes and blacken their faces as a disguise, then enter the household without knocking on the door or even speaking. Humming a hypnotic tune, they began their task of sweeping the room, then when this was completed would hold out their purse for a gift of money. In the cold and darkness the sweepers created a ghostly atmosphere, often frightening small children who thought of them as being bogeymen. Many householders began to resent them entering their homes, so slowly the custom died out.

Seasonal Festivals

At Ashton-under-Lyne an ancient drama was acted out on Easter Monday, known as Shooting the Black Lad. A man dressed as a medieval knight in black armour rode through the town in splendour, but ended up being placed in the pillory. Here he would suffer at the hands of the laughing crowd by being pelted with vegetables and other rubbish.

It is said the custom originates from the 15th century when the locality suffered under the control of a sadistic aristocrat, Ralph of Assheton. As Lord of the Manor he had the right to deal severely with any lawbreakers; a power he used with relish on even trivial offenders. So when his downfall eventually came it was a time for widespread rejoicing, which continued to become an annual celebration. Some believe the custom was much older, as at one time a straw effigy of the knight was said to have been used. This may be a link with a Celtic ceremony, or a renouncing of the old gods which had been replaced by Christianity.

Plough Monday, which is the first Monday after the 6 January, is considered to be the start of the new growing season in rural areas. At this time prayers are offered up for good crops during the coming year. In the village of Bilsborrow, which lies between Preston and Lancaster, the tradition is still followed and the plough is taken into the church to receive a blessing.

The ancient manorial Court leet, held since medieval times at Mitton near Whalley, seems to have died out earlier this century. Local men held this annual event in the Three Fishes Inn, where following a dinner, appointments were made by officers and a jury. These included pounders, pinners, hedgers, ditchers and the all-important ale tester!

A few miles up the Ribble at Grindleton, it was as members of the Hen-Pecked Club that local men vented their feelings on the second Tuesday in June. After being suitably fortified in the village pubs, they would parade through the street, acting out their subservient role, each telling how their wife was boss of their household.

Although we are accustomed to seeing hundreds of bonfires blazing across Lancashire on the fifth of November, in Liverpool Burning Judas was the tradition on Good Friday. Effigies of straw were made by the children who, in the early morning, would carry them in a procession around their local streets chanting, 'Judas is dead'. Long poles were used to rap on the bedroom windows, waking the occupants who would then throw money down. The festivities ended with a bonfire in the street, where Judas was ritually burnt. This became a hazard to residents who, in the 1930s, complained to the police, hoping that they could bring the tradition to an end. In the 1960s the fire brigade was still being called out to extinguish out-of-control Judas Fires, but now the custom seems to have finally died out.

Often motivated by a desire to express religious belief, walking days are a feature of many northern towns. The famous Whit Walks of Manchester draw in thousands of spectators, while Warrington Walking Day has over 6000 people taking part. Started in 1832 by the Revd Powys, it has now grown into a huge inter-denominational event. Colourful banners, music from many different bands, and a marvellous array of flowers create a splendid atmosphere of celebration.

At isolated Bashall Eaves in the Ribble Valley, what was known locally as

Collop Monday preceded Shrove Tuesday. This was the traditional time for farmers to slaughter their pigs so before the austerity of Lent, poor residents of the parish would visit the local farms saying, 'We've come a'colloping,' hoping to be given a few rashers of bacon.

Brindle Cuckoos is the name affectionately given to children born in this lovely village which lies near Chorley. Apparently past villagers decided that if they could prevent the cuckoo from leaving, they would have summer all the year round. Having seen the bird land in a field, they began to build a wall around it, but unfortunately it was not high enough so the bird flew away!

Water Rituals

Due to the unusual drought conditions which have occurred in various parts of England in recent years, water has become newsworthy, yet often it is a commodity which we take for granted. However, it is a vital part of our very existence for although we can survive for several weeks without food, if we are denied water we are dead within days. Over sixty per cent of our body is made up of the compound, so perhaps it is not surprising that our ancestors made it a part of their religious rituals.

When the wanderings of the early nomadic tribes gave way to more permanent settlements, the nearness of a water supply was quite naturally of great importance. This dependence then gave way to superstition, the wells and rivers assuming mystical significance, becoming the abode of water gods who demanded homage. These waters were fed by casting in fruits, blossoms, animals, and even unfortunate humans. Evidence of what is believed to have been a sacrifice to the River Ribble was discovered last century at Preston Docks when a large number of both animal and human skulls were uncovered. As previously mentioned, the Red Moss mummified body of a girl from the first century may well have been a sacrificial virgin who was thrown into the marsh to appease the gods.

In Celtic Lancashire the Druids saw a link between the purity of water and that of the human spirit. Many of their holy places, which later became the sites of our first Christian churches, were built above underground water courses. The paths of these hidden streams closely follow the outline of their ancient shrines, while in the Viking pagan cult of Odinism, the Well of Mirmir became the source of veneration, watering the roots of the sacred ash tree, Yggdrasil.

When the Romans invaded Lancashire during the first century, they brought with them ritualised bathing, a legacy from the priests of Egypt and Persia. They also believed in the healing properties of water which then added another significance to the pagan wells. Later, when Christianity slowly became established, many of these wells were re-dedicated to saints, the water being used for baptism into the new faith. Of singular importance were those associated with Our Lady or St Mary. Water from these wells is still believed by many to possess miraculous powers that can cure people from all types of ailments.

Lancashire's most popular holy well dedicated to Our Lady is at Fernyhalgh, a rural parish which lies north of Preston. A narrow lane passes the church, then continues through green meadowland to the well which stands in the grounds of a large house. Stone steps lead down to the square patch of clear water watched over by the flower-bedecked statue of Our Lady and the Infant Jesus. A legend relates how the well was discovered in 1471 by a merchant who was miraculously saved from a storm while sailing in the Irish Sea. In thanksgiving, he built a chapel close to the well which soon became a place of pilgrimage. This survived until the reign of Kind Edward VI, when it was suppressed and then demolished, but pilgrims still continued to come to the well. In 1685, when religious persecution was less active, a new chapel was built followed by a church in 1796 which has a magnificent fresco-style interior. The well still attracts hundreds of Catholic pilgrims each year who believe the water has curative properties. Other wells dedicated to St Mary existed in Penwortham, Clitheroe and Blackburn.

At Lathom, near Ormskirk, a holy well had an unusual dedication to St Mary Magdalene. It became very popular with the inhabitants of West Lancashire, including the Countess of Derby, who came to take the water. In 1670 a booklet written by Edmund Borlase praised its curative properties, believing it could cure a wide range of diseases from worms to gonorrhoea. Unfortunately, it disappeared last century, being drained into the workings of a mine.

When the Roman Emperor Constantine embraced the Christian faith, many followed his example. He later ordered that the pagan wells should be dedicated to his own mother. St Helen, who had discovered the Holy Cross. At Whittle-le-Woods, near Chorley, a St Helen's well continued to attract pilgrims up to late last century. On the saint's day pins were thrown ceremonially into the water; a link with pagan times. A similar event took place at St Helen's Well at Sefton, where the water was said to possess medicinal properties.

Other saints also frequently associated with holy wells are St Anne, the mother of Our Lady, and St Patrick, the patron saint of Ireland. At remote Inglewhite, near Garstang, there was once a popular St Anne's well which today is almost forgotten. A string of St Patrick's wells, including one at Hest Bank, follow the saint's path from Heysham where he was ship-wrecked, back to his home in the northern Lake District.

In the grounds of ancient Waddow Hall near Clitheroe, now a centre for girl guides, stands sinister Peg o' Nell's Well. Overlooking the fast flowing Ribble and guarded by her headless statue, it has become associated with evil. Every seven years she is said to claim a victim who meets an early death by drowning in the river. Another haunted well house lies in the ruins of

Hollinshead Hall, near Tockholes in the West Pennine Moors, where the water spurts from the mouth of a grotesque gargoyle nicknamed the Spewing Laddie. It is said that a man once lost his mind when locked inside the well house overnight, and many other ghosts have been seen in the ruins.

When the medieval well-dressing ceremony was revived in Tockholes village ten years ago, it brought with it unexpected happenings, but not of the ghostly kind. The act of covering the ancient well near St Stephen's Church with flower pictures and foliage seems to have created a fertility ritual for following the biannual ceremony an unusually large number of the local women found themselves pregnant. The influx of babies was welcomed by the community whose numbers were dwindling, and now women from other areas who are hoping for a family are making a special visit to the well.

It is said that George Fox, founder of the Quaker movement, once stopped to drink at Robin Hood's Well on Pendle Hill before having his famous vision. Below, in the Ribble Valley at Bolton-by-Bowland, the King's Well was discovered by Henry Vl who in 1464 was hiding out at Bolton Hall. A few miles away, on the windswept ridge of Waddington Fell, the icy waters of Walloper Well have been enjoyed for generations by travellers walking to Clitheroe. Only the fit, however, can drink to the memory of Lancashire's famous dialect poet, Edwin Waugh, at the well which is his memorial for it lies high on the isolated moors above the Rossendale Valley, in the landscape which was his inspiration. Those who prefer a more sedate stroll can enjoy a circular walk around the wells and springs of lovely Silverdale. These half-forgotten waters, once so essential to both the animals and villagers, have now been linked by a short circular walk.

Superstitions

In the ancient world religion and superstition had the same meaning; they were concerned with man's desire to unravel the mystery of life and death. Although today we may outwardly scoff at illogical taboos that are reputed to bring bad luck, few of us will deliberately test them by perhaps walking under a ladder or spilling salt. We have inherited these strange superstitions from our ancestors, who believed that seemingly unconnected events affected the outcome of their lives so by being able to read these signs, many of life's tragedies could be avoided.

In the isolated villages of Lancashire there were dozens of different superstitions concerning animals and birds. It was said to be very lucky to see the head of the first lamb of springtime or to see the first cuckoo. On seeing the bird, if you turned your money over, you would never be poor during the rest of the year. House martins and swallows, believed to be God's bow and arrow, also brought good luck if they built their nest on your house, but if bats or frogs entered your cottage, or a bird constantly tapped at your window, misfortune would prevail. Hooting owls and croaking ravens, which were prominent in Norse legends, were also considered unlucky.

In some parts of Lancashire it was firmly believed that the life of a dog was closely bound up with that of its elderly female owner, the death of one was quickly followed by the death of the other, while a dog howling near a door was an omen of death. When a cat started to tear its claws into a cushion or carpet then windy weather would follow. Magpies were generally be-

Magpies are associated with many superstitions

lieved to be unlucky birds who should be dealt with carefully. This was because they were the only birds who refused to enter Noah's Ark, instead they perched on the roof. When seen, to avoid this bad luck, they should be greeted by saying, 'Good morning Magpie'. A rhyme which has many local variations associates the number of birds seen at one time with certain predictions:

One for anger, two for mirth.
Three for a wedding, four for a birth.
Five to be rich, six to be poor.
Seven for a witch, I can tell you no more.

Barnacle geese were once said not to hatch out of an egg, but to be born from a barnacle shell. This led to the conclusion that they were not birds but fish, so as such their flesh could be eaten during Lent! Toads have associations in Lancashire with witchcraft, being generally regarded as symbols of misfortune, but in some localities the opposite is believed.

Robins have always been protected for they are said to have attempted to peck away the nails from Christ's body as he hung on the cross, their breast becoming coloured by his blood. To kill one brings great misfortune, and even to cage one or to break its egg is very bad luck. If a farmer killed one his cows would give blood instead of milk. They are also omens of imminent death if they enter a house or even tap on the window pane, and if they appear to be sheltering in the branches of a tree, then rain will soon fall. Other omens of death include a cock crowing at night or the chance crushing of a beetle underfoot.

Bees, regarded as being the servants of God, are believed to bring bad luck to anyone who kills them, but their sting is a useful cure for rheumatism. It is also a tradition that if the beekeeper dies they must be told about his death. A Lancashire rhyme gives the value of seeing a swarm of bees in different months:

A swarm of bees in May,
Is worth a load of hay.
A swarm of bees n June,
Is worth a silver spoon.
But a swarm in July,
Is not worth a fly.

Other animal superstitions common in Lancashire state that black cats crossing your path and a black lamb born into a flock of white sheep are good omens. Rooks who leave their long established nests, on the other hand, bring misfortune to the land owner, and rats leaving a house mean it is in danger of collapsing.

Money had also many superstitions associated with it, some of which are still common today. When given a cup of tea the number of foamy bubbles that appear on the surface are said to indicate the extent of future wealth. To find a sixpence was considered unlucky unless it was crooked, but coins which were covered with mould were very lucky. Anyone given an object of gold is advised to rub it over both eyelids to acquire yet more wealth.

Many of the Celtic religious practices involved the forest, leading to a host of customs and superstitions associated with trees and plants. In the north the rowan, or mountain ash, is regarded as the most sacred of all the trees. It was used as a protection against witchcraft, its branches being fastened to the doors of barns and shippons. It was also planted close to farms to protect the household from being cursed. The Druids used it in their sacred rituals, while the Norsemen knew it as the earth-tree Yggdrasil, that stretched from heaven to hell.

In parts of Lancashire, including the Fylde, it was a tradition on May Day to light Beltane Fires which it was believed would increase the power of the sun during the following summer. Sacrificial bones were also burnt, from which the term Bone or Bon-fire derived. It was customary during this ceremony to carry rowan twigs as a protection against evil spirits.

Holly is also regarded as a magical tree, having many links with pagan England. The Romans used it at their Saturnalia festival, which later led to its use in our Christmas celebrations. The red berries symbolise Christ's crucifixion and the deep green leaves eternal life, while the prickles ward off evil spirits. Until the last century it was very widely used at Christmas, but when Prince Albert introduced the spruce from Germany, holly lost popularity.

Oak, another ancient sacred tree, was also used in Celtic rituals and looked on with reverence, but it took on a different significance after King Charles II made his famous escape following the Battle of Worcester by hiding in the Royal Oak Tree. Following the Restoration, Oak Apple Day (May 29th) became a holiday widely celebrated in Lancashire, a practice which continued until recent times. Many northern inns boast The Royal Oak on their signs.

The herb rosemary was associated with remembrance, and was once a familiar sight at village funerals. It was placed with the body in the coffin, and also worn in the lapels of mourners. It is still a common practice to touch the hand of the dead person for luck. This custom arose in pagan times when it was believed that a murdered person bled when touched by the murderer, so to touch a corpse was proof of innocence.

Lucky charms to ward off the evil eye and omens which predict death or disaster are a rich part of Lancashire's tradition. In the low-lying areas of the coast, marsh gas, which appeared as a blue light, became known as the corpse light. If it entered the home of a sick person it was a sure sign that death would follow. It was also believed that anyone who watched a church entrance at midnight on St Mark's Eve, would see the faces of those parishioners who were destined to die during the following year.

Any pieces of old iron, horseshoes or rusty nails inside a house were symbols of good luck, but the fireside could reveal misfortune. A cinder when thrown out of the fire indicated a coffin, but if a circular hollow remained in the ashes it meant a purse of gold. A flake of soot on the bars of the grate, or a bright spark in the wick of a candle, indicated the approach of a stranger.

Around the Pendle area, where witchcraft was widely practised, several different charms were used to protect households. Stones which had a natural hole through, known as hag-stones, were commonly thought to ward off evil. A parchment on which was written a charm by a 'wise man', was hidden in barns, while horseshoes, always pointing upwards, had the same effect. If a horseshoe was found in the street it could make a wish come true if spat upon then thrown over the left shoulder!

Lancashire's mining community, living as they once did with the ever-present threat of disaster, were naturally superstitious. They believed it was unlucky for members of the same family to work in the same part of the mine, and they never worked on the first or last day of the year.

Home Cures

Herbal medicine, which in recent years has seen a revival with the spread of health food shops, has for centuries been practised by Lancastrians. Remedies for all manner of ailments were passed down by word of mouth, most of the plants being gathered from the local countryside.

Nettles acted as an expectorant for moving phlegm, but were also used in cooking. Nettle beer became very popular with holidaymakers at Heysham village where it can still be purchased. Dandelions were taken to purify the blood, gentian to cure anaemia, rosemary to remove gas from the bowel and elder to ease headaches. Nearly every household grew its own comfrey plant, known as knitbone, which was used to relieve bruises and strains, and to cure stomach problems. Eyebright soothed painful eyes, feverfew restored a lost appetite and barley-water cleared the kidneys.

At the beginning of winter children had their chests rubbed with goose-grease as a protection against colds, then in spring they were given brimstone and treacle to clear their blood. Cinder tea, made by dropping a hot cinder into water, was used to bring up babies' wind, and a wound healed fast when covered with a clean spider's web. The corner shop also provided a host of popular medicines which included Kaolin and Morphine, Cod Liver Oil and Malt, Indian Brandee, Caster Oil, Oil of Cloves, Camphor and Little Liver Pills.

Herbal Health at Rawtenstall is the last remaining temperance bar in Lancashire. It still does a brisk trade, selling over seventy dried herbs as well as such life-giving drinks from the past as sarsaparilla, dandelion and burdock, camomile tea and black beer.

Chapter Eight

Scales of Justice

Crime and Punishment

Although we have grown accustomed to hearing about the ever-rising crime rate in the north, when we look at our lawless past it soon becomes apparent how fortunate we really are. Following the departure of the Romans, the unprotected tribes which occupied Lancashire became the target for an ever-growing number of invaders from Saxons to Vikings. For centuries it was only the strong who survived; plunder, murder and rape being the order of the day.

Even after the Conquest, the Normans could barely hold their northern territory. The castles at Lancaster and Clitheroe became their strongholds and for centuries had to control what was regarded as being part of a disputed border area. Bands of marauding Scots stole silently south, picking off easy rural targets with bloodthirsty efficiency. This led to the creation of a series of fortified Pele Towers in which vulnerable communities could seek temporary protection, having been pre-warned of the advancing raiders by beacon fires. Turton Tower near Bolton and Arnside Tower north of Lancaster, are survivors from this period.

However, even by the 14th century, when Norman control had become well established in a relatively prosperous country, lawbreaking was still widespread. Gangs of outlaws living in the remote forests continued to prey on towns and villages, killing and robbing at will. In later centuries it was the highwaymen who made travelling a hazardous business. Although social injustice and the power of strong alcohol could perhaps excuse some, in reality most were sadistic thugs. These had freely chosen a criminal life, being prepared to terrorise and murder the innocent to feed their greed.

To cope with lawbreakers the punishments which were devised became equally harsh, seldom showing compassion. Public humiliation, horrific torture and death were commonplace, creating sadistic entertainment for the crowds. The Normans first introduced decapitation as a quick death for the erring aristocrat, originally being carried out by the sword then later the executioner's axe. At Churchgate in Bolton, James, 7th Earl of Derby, suffered this fate in 1651 for his part in the Civil War. The axe fell for the last time in England in 1747, on the neck of the Jacobite Lord Lovat.

Common criminals suffered a slower death by hanging, their bodies often being left for years swinging from the gibbet as a visible deterrent. Traitors were made to suffer most, being hanged until half-dead, then having their bodies mercilessly cut into pieces. This barbaric sentence was carried out on several Roman Catholics during the 17th century at Lancaster, including Saint Edmund Arrowsmith and Saint Ambrose Barlow.

Punishments for more minor offences often involved the use of elaborate apparatus which had evolved over many centuries. The most common were the stocks, in which the legs of offenders were secured through two holes between planks of wood. These open-air prisons were used from the time of Henry III until early last century. Some still survive in Lancashire villages, a fine example can be seen on the green at Rivington.

The village stocks at Rivington

The Brank or Gossip's Bridle was a device made from metal strips which was locked around the head. An attached plate was lodged in the mouth clamping the tongue, making speech impossible. Those sentenced, often by the local house of correction, were mainly woman who had been found guilty of gossiping. Branks were to be found throughout Lancashire, including Manchester, Lancaster, Kirkham, and Preston, which possessed two of the devices. At Warrington the last victim was Cicily Pewsill, a notorious scold from the local workhouse who was forced to wear the device in the street.

Death by drowning was originally a punishment administered by the Celts, the offenders being submerged beneath the water in a wooden cage. By Saxon times this had evolved into the cucking or ducking stool: an open-bottomed chair which hung from a pivoted beam, allowing the secured offender to be ducked into a pond or river. The intention was to douse and humiliate the victims who were mainly women, but occasionally the punishment led to drowning. Ducking stools were used throughout Lancashire, including Manchester where it was placed beside the Infirmary Ponds, and Liverpool where it stood in the grounds of the appropriately named Hellhole Prison. At Woodplumpton near Preston the former site of the punishment is remembered in the name of Cuckstool Farm.

Every Norman castle had its dungeons, but the first record of a prison for thieves was at Winchester in 1103. Lancaster Castle became Lancashire's main jail, but imprisonment was generally regarded as an interim measure before punishment was administered. Later, prisons, lock-ups and houses of correction were built in other towns. A unique reminder of local justice can still be seen behind the Old Dungeon Inn at Tottington, near Bury. Here a solid stone dungeon was built in 1835 to lock up drunks.

Penal reform in England began during the early 19th century, slowly ending a legacy of barbarism which stretched back to prehistoric times. The last public execution took place in 1868 at Newgate, and the last hard-labour treadmill was suspended in 1902. England's last hanging took place in Lancashire on the 13 August 1964, when two men were executed on the same day. Peter Anthony Allen died at Walton Prison, Liverpool, and John Robson Walby was hanged at Strangeways Gaol in Manchester. Corporal punishment in prisons ended in 1962 and the death penalty for murder was finally abolished in 1969.

Hanging Town

The city of Lancaster, situated as it is on the side of the Lune and filled with a host of historical connections, has quite naturally become a popular escape for tourists. They saunter down to St George's Quay, explore the lovely Priory Church of St Mary, then perhaps discover the elegant splendour of the Ashton Memorial. However, few are aware that their visit is perpetuating an ancient, yet more gory tradition – in the past up to 6000 visitors would flock into the city in a single day to watch the bloody spectacle of a public execution in the Hanging Town.

It is the grim, grey-stoned castle, which is still used as a prison, court and museum, that lies at the centre of Lancaster's notorious executions. Standing on a former Roman fort, this Norman stronghold was built by Roger of Poitou in 1093 on a magnificent hilltop site. In 1168 the newly formed county of Lancaster embraced much of his former lands. Two centuries later the dukedom of Lancaster was created, and since 1399 the title has been held by the reigning monarch. Consequently, during the last 900 years the castle has seen many royal visitors including King John, Edward II, John of Gaunt, Henry IV, Edward IV, James I and Queen Victoria.

No doubt these privileged visitors would be entertained in lavish style, but for those who broke the strict laws of the past a less attractive fate awaited in the dank, rat-infested castle dungeons. A row of these claustrophobic cells remain, lying inside the solid curtain walls which are over nine feet thick. Measuring just ten feet square, up to sixty prisoners would lie in total darkness behind the solid oak doors. Fed just once a day and lying in their own filth, for even basic sanitation was denied them, death would perhaps seem an easy option to many of these diseased prisoners.

Prior to 1796 executions took place on a site named Golgotha which lies on the road to Lancaster Moor, on the outskirts of the city. Traditionally, prisoners were allowed to stop for their last drink at the Golden Lion pub which still stands in Moor Lane. Of the many hundreds of prisoners who took this grim path over 700 years, only a few names survive. Many were murderers and thieves, others were accused of witchcraft and sorcery, while a few were willing to die rather than renounce their religious beliefs.

Following the Dissolution of the Monasteries, two of the first men to pay the supreme price for their faith were Abbot John Paslew of Whalley Abbey and Abbot William Trafford of Salley Abbey. They had opposed Henry VIII's autocratic rule by joining the rebellion known as the Pilgrimage of Grace. In 1554, when for a short period Queen Mary restored the Catholic faith, Protestant George Marsh of Bolton was imprisoned at Lancaster, then he was later horribly burnt to death at Chester.

The reign of Elizabeth brought with it a period of Roman Catholic persecution that was to last over a century. Among those who died at Lancaster were: Blessed Edward Thwing (1600), Bld Robert Nutter (1600), Bld Robert Middleton (1601), Bld Thurstan Hunt (1601), Bld John Thules (1616), Bld Roger Wrenno (1616), Saint Edmund Arrowsmith (1628), Saint Ambrose Barlow (1641), Bld Edward Bamber (1646) and Bld John Woodcock (1646). In most cases these martyrs fearlessly faced a terrible death by being hanged, drawn and quartered. Parts of their bodies were then displayed on the castle walls.

The notorious period of the witch hunt also began during the reign of Elizabeth, then reached its height when James I came to the throne. Edward Hartley was one of the first alleged witches to suffer at Lancaster in 1597, to be followed in 1612 by the famous Pendle brood. They were held in a dungeon which is still in existence, its walls having been made of river mud. Marks which are visible on the damp walls are believed to have been made by the clawing fingernails of the prisoners. They paid the price for their occult practices on the 20 August 1612 when they were hung in front of a huge crowd.

George Fox, the founder of the Quaker movement, was no stranger to the inside of English prisons and he knew the dungeons of Lancaster well. In 1652 he was fortunate in being acquitted when accused of voicing his outlawed religious beliefs, but for a period in 1660 he was imprisoned, and a longer term of two years followed in 1663. The brave woman who later became his wife, Margaret Fell, spent four and a half years imprisoned at the castle, which at this time was full of her fellow Quakers. On her release she journeyed throughout England, comforting some of the 4000 Quakers who had been jailed, many of whom died before completing their sentences. The Quakers' Room at the castle stand as a memorial to their suffering.

Old Ned

The impressive Shire Hall and Crown Court, which stands within Lancaster Castle, was built in 1798. Around its walls are mounted a colourful array of coats-of-arms, and a formidable arrangement of weapons which were once used to guard judges and High Sheriffs. No doubt these officials needed protection for the law in Lancaster was administered with an iron fist. The court gained an unenviable reputation of having sentenced more people to death than any other in England. This reached a height during the early 19th century when 240 people were condemned during a short four year period, but thankfully, most of these were later reprieved.

Of all the hangmen of Lancaster who carried out the unsavoury task of giving the criminals their 'just deserts', none was more hated than Edward 'Old Ned' Barlow. A Welshman by birth, he gleefully took up the position in 1781 when he was aged 45, and over the next 30 years ended the life of 131 criminals. Regarded by most as being as bad as his victims, he was shunned by the local people and was 'often pelted with missiles of the foulest description' and 'not infrequently was he rolled in the mud.'

Old Ned's day began in the Drop Room where the condemned prisoner was brought from the chapel to be pinioned, accompanied by the melancholy sound of the prison bell. From here large doors opened out into that part of the castle which became known as Hanging Corner. In the early days the rope was attached to a simple beam which protruded from above the open doors. The noose was placed around the criminal's neck, then he was pushed outwards to hang until dead, which sometimes took up to twenty minutes. On occasions a condemned man would pay children as 'hangers on' or 'to pull their leg', which meant that they clung on to the hanging body to add extra weight which resulted in a quick death. The dead body was then lowered before being pushed backwards into a cellar where it was retrieved and placed in a coffin. It was then often buried in an unmarked grave close to the present wall of the nearby church.

Later the procedure became more sophisticated with the erection of a gallows which had a stout cross-beam. In 1817 Old Ned, ever-boastful of his technique, had his greatest triumph. He hung nine criminals at the same time, five of whom were not yet twenty-years-old. He was still trying to live down the disappointment of 1791 when James Burns, who was awaiting execution, managed to commit suicide in the condemned cell. Having cheated the hangman, the public were still determined that he would not escape entirely. A long procession carried his body up to Lancaster Moor, then a stake was driven through his heart before burial.

Thousands of people flocked to Lancaster from all parts of the north on Hanging Day, which came to be regarded as a holiday. The gentry paid to get a grandstand view from the church roof, while the Grammar School allowed its pupils the morning free from lessons so they could watch the event. Old Ned was also sure of making 'money for old rope' by cutting up the noose and selling the pieces to the visitors who used them as lucky charms.

In 1806, however, the old inns of Lancaster were buzzing with a story that brought a smile to many faces: for the callous hangman had been charged with horse stealing. This carried a death penalty so the possibility arose that he may be hung from his own gallows. Although he was eventually found guilty of the offence, his sentence was commuted to ten years in jail for his expertise was in great demand. He was confined to the prison, but continued to carry out his duties as normal.

As well as being the hangman, Ned's other jobs included flogging, whipping and branding. The latter took place in open court where a criminal would be branded with a letter 'M' for malefactor or 'V' for vagabond as a method of identifying that he had a criminal record. His hand would be secured in a device known as a holdfast, then a red-hot branding iron would be used to imprint the letter on his thumb. When Old Ned was satisfied that the print was legible he would announce, 'A fair mark, my Lord.' Sometimes the letter was branded on the criminal's heel, from which the term 'showing a clean pair of heels' evolved. The branding iron and the holdfast, which is still kept in the court, were last used in 1811. Old Ned died at the castle where he had worked for so long and was buried in the churchyard, close to the many criminals he had dispatched.

From this era of morbid curiosity and ghoulish callousness tales of both great tragedy and black humour have survived. In 1831 a man awaiting execution was determined to prove his own mother wrong. From early childhood, due to his wayward ways, she had told him he would never die with his boots off. As he mounted the scaffold it looked as if she was going to be proved right, until in a last act of defiance he managed to kick them off, and presumably died satisfied.

Just three years earlier the pathetic figure of Jane Scott, an eighteen-year-old girl from Preston, had entered the Drop Room. Having been found guilty of poisoning both her parents, she was about to face the hangman. Unable to walk, the crippled girl had to be pushed in a special wheel chair to the scaffold aided by two female prisoners. At the final second they were given the signal to step aside before she took the last drop. Her body was then given to a surgeon to carry out medical dissection and in later years her skeleton was displayed in a house in her home town.

Transportation to the penal colonies in Australia was also a punishment given at times for crimes which would now be considered trivial and women sentenced to hard labour were forced to walk endlessly upon a treadmill which was used to grind corn. Twenty-two rooms were filled by people who could not pay their debts, but they were charged 'room money' for using the castle facilities. The last public execution at Lancaster took place in 1865 and the last hanging inside the castle was in 1911. The castle prison, after nine centuries, is scheduled to close, but the court, which in recent years saw the widely publicised trial of the Birmingham Six, is still in use.

Perhaps the reputation of Old Ned motivated other Lancastrians to take up the career of hangman for the county has provided many well-known executioners. When the present century dawned it was Boltonian James Billington, often aided by his sons Thomas and William, who was England's chief hangman. A barber by trade, he travelled throughout the country carrying out the ultimate punishment wherever the law demanded it. Following his death in 1901 he was succeeded by William, who had the distinction of carrying out the last hanging at notorious Newgate Prison. This took place in May 1901 when a soldier, George Woolfe, was executed for the murder of his former girlfriend.

John Ellis, a Rochdale millworker who later became a barber, was another prominent hangman of this period, often assisting the famous Henry Pierrepoint. In 1910 he hanged Doctor Crippen, who was the first murderer to be captured using the new wireless communication as he tried to escape by ship to Canada. Ellis also executed George Smith, who was known as the 'Brides in the Bath' murderer, in 1915, and Sir Roger Casement, who had been found guilty of treason, in 1916.

In 1906 William Willis from Accrington became Ellis's assistant, working at the 'trade' until 1926. Other Lancashire hangmen include Henry Pollard (Blackburn), Lionel Mann (Rochdale), Thomas Phillips (Farnworth) and Robert Wilson (Manchester).

Death of a Packman

In summertime, the heathery moors which rise up to the high summit of Winter Hill are tranquil and beautiful. Larks soar upwards into the blue sky, curlews glide in the warm air currents, while in all directions can be seen a magnificent panorama of unspoilt countryside. But walkers who venture across this part of Lancashire's West Pennine Moors are reminded of a less peaceful episode in the area's history for a unique memorial, known locally as the Scotsman's Stump, tells of a terrible murder which took place here during the last century:

'In memory of George Henderson, traveller,
native of Annan, Dunfrieshire, who was
barbarously murdered on Rivington Moor at
noonday, November 9th 1838 in the 20th year
of his age.'

The murder victim was a packman who was employed by William Jardine, a Blackburn draper. It was his job to travel on foot through Lancashire selling and delivering his employer's goods, and collecting payments. He followed regular routes, which on the fateful day involved crossing Horwich and Rivington Moor on his way home to Blackburn.

At that time, an isolated row of cottages known as Five Houses stood on the side of the moor. One was a beerhouse and Henderson had arranged to meet up at this hostelry with his fellow packman, Benjamin Birrell, at 11 o'clock so they could walk to Blackburn together. Henderson failed to arrive so Birrell decided to leave without him, asking the landlord's wife, Mrs Garbutt, to tell Henderson of his departure. Birrell later recalled that as he walked across the moor he spoke to a man carrying a gun for shooting birds and who appeared to be acting strangely.

Henderson arrived at Five Houses at noon, but learning that his colleague had left, he quickly continued on his way. A young boy named Thomas Whowell was slowly riding a horse along the same route at this time, taking a meal to his brother who worked in a nearby mine. The boy was finding the animal difficult to control so he swore at it, which caused Henderson to rebuke him.

After delivering the food to the mine, the boy was returning along the track when he was shocked to come upon a pool of blood, then he heard terrible moans coming from a ditch. Frightened, he ran for help to James Fletcher who was busy working at a nearby coal outcrop. Fletcher immediately came to his aid, finding Henderson lying face upwards in a ditch suffering from terrible wounds. One of his eyes had been completely blown away by a bullet, while the other lay horribly out of its socket resting on his cheek. With help from others, Fletcher carried Henderson the half mile to the Five Houses beerhouse and a doctor was called, but sadly the young Scotsman died less than two hours later.

The crime gained a great deal of publicity throughout Lancashire, with Henderson's employer, William Jardine, offering a reward of £100 for any information which would lead to a conviction. An inquest was held in the Horwich Moorgate Inn, which is now the popular Blundell Arms pub, where circumstantial evidence pointed the finger at a local collier, 22-year-old James Whittle. Although Birrell was unable to positively identify Whittle as the man he saw carrying the gun, the inquest was told that he had a single barrelled rifle in his possession, loaned by the landlord of the Horwich Moorgate Inn. After hearing the evidence for two days, the inquest returned a verdict of 'wilful murder' against Whittle, who was ordered to stand trial.

A large crowd watched in shocked silence as the funeral cortège of George Henderson wound its way from Horwich to Blackburn on the 14th November 1838. The service took place in the packed Presbyterian Chapel in Mount Street. His sister, who had travelled down from Scotland, represented the family as the chief mourner.

Six months later, on the 2nd April 1839, the trial was held at Liverpool

James Whittle, who was accused of killing the packman

Crown Court. The main witness for the prosecution was Joseph Halliwell, who was employed by a Bolton cattle dealer. He related how he heard the sound of a gunshot while travelling across the moor, then shortly afterwards saw Whittle carrying the weapon. His aggressive manner and contradictory statements during cross-examination alienated the jury and lost the prosecution the case. After just one day a verdict of 'Not Guilty' was reached and Whittle was given his freedom, the judge remarking that the jury had taken the safest side.

On the rugged moorland at the site of the crime, a tree was planted as a memorial to George Henderson. Over the years it was cut away by souvenir hunters, its remains becoming known as the Scotsman's Stump. In 1912 a group of Bolton business men subscribed to a replacement cast iron pillar and plaque, which now stands close to the soaring TV mast which dominates the area.

Although James Whittle was freed, the murder remaining unsolved, he was ostracised by many during his lifetime. In later years he became blind, dying at the age of 54 in 1872, and being laid to rest in Horwich parish church graveyard.

The Manchester Martyrs

St Joseph's Roman Catholic Cemetery at Moston, which originally covered 5.75 hectares (14 acres), was first established in 1874. It was set up by the bishop who had to face the ever-increasing problem of burying the Catholic dead in bustling Victorian Manchester, a city which was expanding its boundaries in all directions. The small churchyard burial grounds which at this time existed in the city centre were becoming full, with some being prone to flooding from the River Medlock. Bodies were occasionally washed away, leading to the danger of spreading such water-borne diseases as ty-

The Manchester Martyrs memorial, Moston cemetery

phoid and cholera, which were a curse of the age. By 1896 it was clear that the cemetery would not be adequate, and its size was doubled to 11.5 hectares (28 acres) – yet it is estimated that in 14 years time it will be completely full.

Today the cemetery has become recognised as an important and unique link with the Victorian age. Here Manchester's Blue Badge Guides take visitors around both the ornate marble and simple stone monuments marking the graves of an international community. Towering Italian tombs with finely sculptured statues and photos of the dead occupants line the 'posh' part, while a sea of austere slabs, each recording up to twelve names, marks the final resting place of the poor. Such was the depth of these that on seeing an empty grave one observer said it 'stretched right down to Hell itself'.

However, standing alongside the final resting place of both the famous and the unknown, is one of Lancashire's most controversial structures. This large monument to the Manchester Martyrs remembers not those who died for their faith, as the name might suggest, but three members of the Irish Republican Brotherhood (IRB), known as the Fenians, who were the forerunners of the IRA and who died for home rule!

It has been estimated that almost a third of Manchester's population during the last century were of Irish origin. These were mainly the poor, many of whom had survived the horrors of famine, and had arrived in the city seeking work. Although under the law they were now allowed to practise their Catholic faith, in reality there was much opposition, particularly from the non-conformist groups. In 1852 there was even an anti-Catholic riot in Stockport.

In March 1867 two leading members of the undercover IRB had been arrested in Manchester for their part in the separatist movement. During the following September they were being transported through the city in a horse-drawn prison van when it was ambushed by thirty of their group. This occurred on Hyde Road, close to a railway arch which is still known as the Fenian Arch. A bullet is said to have been fired at the lock of the van, but this passed through the keyhole, killing a police sergeant who was guarding the prisoners. The pair managed to escape, but the whole incident brought a wave of fury throughout the country.

Three of the men involved in the plot – William Allen, Michael Larkin and Michael O'Brien – were arrested, and in November 1867, in spite of little evidence, they were sentenced to death at a special court. They were later publicly hanged outside the New Baily prison, guarded by row upon row of armed soldiers. Although they are believed to have taken part in the raid, it was said by their supporters that the death of the policeman was an accident and none of the three actually fired the shot. One tale relates how the IRB member responsible escaped to the USA and many years later, in Philadelphia, made a deathbed confession.

The whole incident caused a great amount of unrest throughout the worldwide Irish community, with the three quickly becoming termed The

Manchester Martyrs. Their death was a focal point for the Irish home rule campaign, a song written in their honour entitled *God Save Ireland* becoming the anthem of the IRB. Such was the depth of feeling of the Irish Catholics of Manchester that, despite the opposition of the bishop, the martyrs' monument was erected at the heart of Moston Cemetery.

Bill's O' Jack's Killings

The lonely Moor Cock Inn, which lay alongside the Greenfield-Holmfirth road on the side of Saddleworth Moor, served its last pint on the 20 April 1937. It was later demolished, leaving today just a few tumbled stones which outline the windswept site, but curious visitors still come here, intent on seeking out the place where one of the most sensational murders of the last century was committed in 1832.

The inn was known locally as Bill's o' Jack's, named after its former landlord Jack Bradbury, who had passed his licence over to his son Bill. But at this time the well-liked owner was himself 86 years old, so he relied heavily

The old Moor Cock Inn, Saddleworth

on his 47-year-old son, Thomas, to run the pub. The pair also owned the shooting rights for part of the moor, which provided them with extra income, but was a worry as it was constantly targeted by poachers.

On the evening of 2 April 1832 one of the regular customers drinking at the inn was Reuben Platt, a local man, well-known in the isolated community. When he was about to leave, Thomas Bradbury decided to walk with him down the moorland road as he needed to buy provisions from Whitehead's Store which lay near Platt's home. Leaving the old man alone, the two men set off. After walking a short distance they met three rough-looking Irishmen who were resting on the roadside. One of these asked how far it was to Holmfirth, and Thomas told them it was eight miles. The three then began to walk up the road which would take them past the inn.

After visiting the store, Thomas began the return journey in the inky darkness. As he approached the inn he was guided by the yellow candle light which came from the windows, but he was unprepared for the horrific sight which met his eyes inside the building. His father, who had been savagely attacked, lay dreadfully wounded on the floor. Then he, too, became the subject of a vicious onslaught by several hidden thugs. Being fit and muscular, he put up a strong defence, but he was unable to withstand the combined effects of an array of weapons which included a spade, a poker, an auger and a pistol butt. Soon he, too, was lying in a crimson pool of his own blood.

It was half-past ten on the following morning before the horrific crime was discovered by Bill's ten-year-old granddaughter, Amelia Winterbottom. She ran for help to James Whitehead who returned with his wife to the inn. Doctor Sam Higginbottom of Uppermill was summoned, but despite all efforts he was unable to save the two victims. Tom, whose head had fifteen gashes and whose skull was fractured, died without regaining consciousness a few hours later. His father, who had been mercilessly beaten on his legs, hands and face, died the following day.

The ferocity of the callous attack sent shock waves around the area. An inquest held at the King William pub at Uppermill the following week, returned a verdict of, 'Wilful murder against some person or persons at present unknown'. A reward of £100 was then offered for any information which would lead to a conviction.

For months the police carried out extensive enquiries into the murders, seeking out the Irishmen who were the main suspects. Others, including James and Joe Bradbury, known as the Red Bradburys, who were not related to the victims, were apprehended near Huddersfield as 'suspicious' but were later released. Two others ruffians were later interviewed at Liverpool, but these, too, were discharged. Even Reuben Platt was regarded as a suspect, but no real evidence against him existed. The police investigation eventually came to an end having found little success – the ghastly murder remaining on the files as 'unsolved'.

But in spite of the passage of time, interest in the Bill's O' Jack's killings lives on. For over a century crowds poured into the isolated inn, drawn by curiosity to the scene of the unsolved crime, and still many visit the site. Only in recent years has it been overshadowed by an even more horrific crime for by a strange twist of fate the evil Moors Murderers buried one of their child victims just a mile from the former pub.

Crimes of Passion

The 1930s saw two famous murder cases in Lancashire which attracted national attention. The police quickly brought one of the murderers to justice, but the second crime remains unsolved.

Doctor Buck Ruxton was a Parsee Indian of mixed French-Indian blood who gained his medical degrees at Bombay University. After undertaking further study in Edinburgh and London, he set up a practice in Lancaster in 1930. Well-dressed, flamboyant and volatile by nature, with his Scottish-born wife Isabelle at his side, his greatest desire was to be accepted by Lancaster's social set of the day. But although within five years he had the trappings of middle-class wealth, owning a large car and a house in prestigious Dalton Square, he still remained an outsider.

In fact, the Ruxtons were not actually married to each other, but merely lived together. Isabelle had been married in 1919 to a Dutchman, but this relationship had failed. She then fell in love with the attractive Bukhtyar Hakim, who changed his name to the more acceptable Buck Ruxton. By 1935 they had three young children, Elizabeth, Diane and William, but Isabelle had not settled down to domestic bliss. Instead she pursued the good life, becoming an active member of Lancaster's young in-crowd. This led to her having a string of sexual affairs which became common knowledge in the town.

Perhaps due to the strain of his seemingly empty life with a wife who had drifted away from him, Buck Ruxton's mind eventually snapped. In a bout of frenzied horror he murdered both Isabelle and their maid, Mary Rogerson. Using his surgical knowledge, he then proceeded to cut up their bodies, parcelling up the dismembered limbs in newspaper. Driving northwards towards Edinburgh, he disposed of the gruesome packages at various places along his route. Some were tossed into wayside ditches and others probably buried.

It was close to the aptly named Devil's Bridge at Moffat that parts of the women's bodies were sensationally discovered. The newspaper in which they were wrapped provided a vital clue which quickly led back to Lancaster. Clever forensic evidence later identified the heads as belonging to the two women who had been reported missing. This inevitably led to the arrest of the doctor, then his subsequent trial which was reported throughout the world.

The jury took just one hour to reach a verdict of guilty. On the 12 May

1936 Buck Ruxton was hanged at Strangeways Gaol in Manchester, and his innocent children had lost both their parents. The crime scene, his former home at 2 Dalton Square, in the heart of Lancaster, then remained unoccupied for half a century.

At the same time that Buck Ruxton was suffering the torments of his lost love affair, the isolated Ribble Valley hamlet of Bashall Eaves became the unlikely setting for another murder. In March 1934 an event took place down one of its leafy lanes which still baffles criminologists. It is also said that the victim's ghost awaits justice.

Farmer John Dawson, who was unmarried, lived with his sister in the hamlet. One Sunday evening he returned home from his usual visit to the local pub at about 10pm, ate the supper his sister had left for him then retired to bed. Early the next morning his sister was startled to hear him shouting out loudly for her help. She hurried to his bedroom to find he was lying on the bed in deep pain. He quickly told her what had happened. On the previous evening, during his walk home, as he opened a field gate he suddenly felt something strike him in the back. Briefly it had hurt him, but this quickly passed so he soon dismissed the incident, but now the pain had returned. His sister saw patches of blood on the bed-sheets, then when she examined his back was horrified to find a gaping wound. A doctor was immediately called who, on seeing the injury, which he identified as a gun-shot wound, had Dawson taken to hospital. The police were then notified.

After three days in hospital the unfortunate victim died, having given no clue to who had shot him. A post-mortem examination revealed that a home-made bullet had penetrated Dawson's shoulder, then had continued into his liver, causing massive internal damage which had led to his death.

The thorough police investigation which followed met a wall of silence from the local close-knit community. John Dawson seemed to have no obvious enemies, he was not robbed, so no real motive was identified. The strange murder still officially remains on police files as unsolved. In more recent years it has been suggested that it resulted from a clandestine love affair which was known about in the valley; his unknown murderer being driven into a crime of passion.

However, John Dawson's ghost still seems intent on justice for many local people claim to have seen it close to the spot where he was shot. The apparition, which has his pronounced stocky figure, wears a blood-stained coat and appears to be searching for clues in a hedgerow.

The Moors Murderers

The magnificent brown moorland which rises to the east of Oldham is among the wildest in Britain. Separating Lancashire from Yorkshire, these windswept Pennine hills sweep outwards like a vast peaty sea, broken only by the occasional line of a drystone wall. Here curlews and larks rise in early springtime, peregrine falcons skim like Tornado jets through the clear air and small groups of tough hillwalkers trek in determined fashion along the Pennine Way.

From the village of Greenfield, the A635 ascends steeply, curving its way through this windswept wilderness in the direction of Holmfirth. Many visitors are tempted to stop at the high point of the road to admire the stunning view. Below lies the blue expanse of the Dovestone Reservoirs set in a deep-cut valley, surrounded by the ever-present hills. But this idyllic spot has become forever tarnished in the eyes of the world for a glance at the map reveals it to be Saddleworth Moor, the spot chosen by the evil Moors Murderers, Ian Brady and Myra Hindley, to bury their child victims. Three bodies have so far been found here and at least one more is believed to still lie hidden, a terrible legacy from the horrific events that unfolded three decades ago.

It was a phone call received at Hyde Police Station in Manchester at 6.10am on the 7 October 1965 that began the terrible affair. The frightened caller, speaking from a telephone box in a street in Hattersley, was 17-year-old David Smith and he was reporting a murder. A police car rushed to the telephone box, where both Smith and his wife, Maureen, were picked up. The couple were then taken to the police station where, in a state of nervous agitation, David Smith told astonished officers how he had seen his sister-in-law's boyfriend, Ian Brady, smash the skull of a boy with a hatchet. This had taken place in the living room of a council house in Wardle Brook Avenue in Hattersley just a few hours earlier.

Acting on this information, detectives Superintendent Bob Talbot and Sergeant Carr immediately organised a police raid on the premises. Disguised with a white overall borrowed from a baker who was delivering bread in the area, Superintendent Talbot knocked on the door of the house. It was opened by Myra Hindley, Maureen Smith's sister, who, off guard, put up no resistance when the policeman revealed his true identity. Once inside the officers found two other occupants, Hindley's boyfriend, 23-year-old Ian Brady, and her invalid grandmother, who was in bed in an upstairs bedroom.

A search of the house then revealed that Smith's allegation was true: wrapped in a blanket within a locked upstairs room was discovered the body of a boy. This was later identified as being 17-year-old Edward Evans, an apprentice who worked at Trafford Park and lived with his parents in Ardwick. Brady was arrested the same day, followed by Hindley four days later. As the investigation continued over the following weeks, the true extent of their evil crimes slowly became apparent.

An exercise book found in the house had the name of John Kilbride written inside. He was a 12-year-old boy who was missing from his home in Ashton-under-Lyne. But two suitcases which had been placed in the left-luggage office at Manchester Central Railway Station contained the most damning evidence. Among sadistic devices and pornographic photos were some horrific audio tapes. These recorded the last poignant moments in the life of a small 10-year-old girl, Lesley Ann Downey, who had disappeared from a funfair at Ancoats in 1964. She was being assaulted by two people before being mercilessly strangled to death.

On the 21 October 1965, now with significantly more evidence, the police officially charged the couple. Brady was accused of murdering Evans, Kilbride and Downey, while Hindley was also charged with the murder of Evans and Downey, and being an accessory to the murder of Kilbride. Six months later, on the 19 April 1966, in the full glare of world publicity, the sensational trial was opened at Chester. As it proceeded, the chance events which led to the evil couple meeting each other then becoming accomplices in such hideous killings was revealed.

Brady, the illegitimate son of a waitress, had been born in the Gorbals area of Glasgow in 1938. He became the foster child of the Sloan family, retaining the surname Stewart which was the name of his mother. He proved to be a difficult child, becoming involved in house breaking from an early age with hints of sadistic behaviour. When he was almost seventeen, the courts placed him on probation, ordering him to live with his natural mother who had married a man named Brady and was living in Manchester.

He moved south to Lancashire in 1954, taking the new surname of Brady, and obtained a job as a porter at Smithfield Market. About this time he became an ardent collector of Nazi memorabilia, with an unhealthy interest in the pornographic works of de Sade. Two years later his criminal activities once more surfaced: he was found guilty of handling stolen goods which resulted in him being given two years in Borstal. In 1959, having served his sentence, he returned to Manchester where he obtained a job as a clerk at Millwards soap factory in Gorton.

In comparison Myra Hindley had a normal childhood. She had been born in 1942 in Manchester, the daughter of Bob Hindley and Hettie Maybury. They lived in Eaton Street in Gorton, her father working in the building trade and her mother as a machinist. Home life was far from settled for her father was a heavy drinker and this often led to bouts of violence when he beat his wife. To escape these violent outbursts she would go to the home of her loving grandmother who lived alone in nearby Bannock Street. After the birth of her sister Maureen in 1946 this became her permanent home.

She was well-liked locally, being regarded as a normal if exuberant girl, with no indication of the evil traits which were to follow. At the age of 15 she started work as a clerk in a local factory, then the following year she returned to the Catholic faith that she had originally been born into. The cinema, the dance hall and thoughts of marriage filled her spare time and at the age of seventeen she became engaged to a local boy named Ronnie Sinclair. However, their relationship failed to blossom and they parted. This was followed by another blow when she was made redundant from her job.

In January 1961 Myra Hindley took up another position as a shorthand typist at Millwards soap factory, where on her first day she met Ian Brady. Almost immediately she became infatuated by his hard, but strangely compelling presence. At first he did not respond then, following an office party, they went out on their first date. Soon they were lovers, with Hindley becoming ever more spellbound by the man she found hypnotic. All her former religious beliefs quickly melted away, being replaced by his atheistic, Nazi and criminal views. These she embraced with relish, indulging in pornographic photo studies with him and providing encouragement for his every whim. For years, he confided, he had yearned to carry out a massive crime. At first, it is believed he had considered carrying out a bank robbery, then chillingly his psychopathic mind decided on murder. With Myra Hindley he had found a willing partner.

The full, horrific details of what followed during the next few years were revealed to a startled jury. Children had been snatched from the street, subjected to sadistic torture, mercilessly killed, then buried in hidden graves. The bodies of Lesley Anne Downey and John Kilbride were discovered on Saddleworth Moor in October 1965. Only when Brady attempted to enlist David Smith as another accomplice was the gruesome plan revealed to the police. On the 6 May 1966 the sensational trial came to an end with both Brady and Hindley, now known forever as the Moors Murderers, being found guilty and sent to jail for life.

But the case was far from complete for the fate of two other missing children, Pauline Reade and Keith Bennett, remained unresolved. It was twenty years before Hindley and Brady finally admitted that they, too, had been their victims. The head of Greater Manchester CID, Peter Topping, brought Hindley and Brady, separately, back to Saddleworth Moor to try to point out where the hidden graves lay. The body of Pauline Reade was eventually found on the moor in 1987 but an exhaustive attempt to find Keith Bennett proved unsuccessful.

The two evil murderers have now served over thirty years in jail. Despite appeals from fervent Christian, Lord Longford, who believes Hindley is a reformed person, public opinion makes it unlikely that she will ever be released.

Chapter Nine

Disasters

The Sinking of the Titanic

Overlooking the choppy grey water of the Mersey on Liverpool's renowned waterfront is a unique monument which has the unusual title of the Memorial to the Engine-room Workers. Cut in white granite, its sculptured panels show a greaser stripped to the waist, a stoker with his shovel and other workmen holding spanners and crowbars. It is a fitting reminder of the price paid by so many Lancashire men who died in the engine room and lower decks of the ill-fated *Titanic* in 1912. For this, perhaps the most publicised of all maritime disasters, has many tragic connections with the county.

The *Titanic* was built in Belfast by Harland and Wolff for the White Star Line, and was launched on 31 May 1911. This magnificent passenger liner, sister to *The Olympic,* was the largest and most opulent in the world. After being completed early in 1912 she left Belfast for sea trials, then proceeded

The ill-fated Titanic was launched on the 31st May, 1911

to Southampton to take on passengers for her maiden voyage to New York. In charge of the huge liner was bearded Captain Edward Smith, the senior captain of the White Star Line, a striking figure with over thirty-eight years service with the company.

At noon on the 10th April 1912, the 882 feet long giant left the crowds behind at Southampton, setting a course first for Cherbourg then for Queenstown in Ireland to pick up other passengers. Among the 2207 people on board were some of the richest and most glamorous in the world. These included multi-millionaire Colonel J.J. Astor, White Star Line chairman Bruce Ismay, Lady Cosmo Duff-Gordon, journalist W.T. Stead and the Countess of Rothes. These first-class passengers were housed in elegant splendour, their luxurious staterooms boasting every facility of the age. For five days they enjoyed the marvellous atmosphere that prevailed in this remarkable vessel, secure in the knowledge that it was said to be unsinkable.

Aware of warnings of ice, the watch on board *Titanic* on the evening of the 14 April had nothing unusual to report until almost 11.40pm. Then suddenly, as if from nowhere, a towering wall of ice came into view. Immediately the signal bell was rung three times and the bridge was informed. The ship veered to port but it was too late, a collision with the 100 feet high iceberg was inevitable. Captain Smith ordered the emergency doors to be closed, hoping the damage would be minimal, but sadly this was not the case. The cold Atlantic water began to cascade through a gash in the hull. Five minutes after midnight the order was given to muster the crew and passengers, and to uncover the lifeboats. Then followed a wireless call for help and the firing of rockets.

About ten miles away from the stricken vessel the small, 6000 ton Leyland Liner *Californian* was motionless, stopped by the drifting ice. Her 35-year-old captain was Stanley Lord, a Bolton-born mariner who had made his first voyage at the age of thirteen. Among his crew were twelve other Lancashire men, including Chief Mate G.F. Stewart from Liverpool and Apprentice James Gibson from Southport. At 11.10pm Third Officer Groves had seen the lights of a large ship passing fast, this he reported to Captain Lord who told him to try to make contact by morse lamp. At 11.40 Groves noticed that most of the lights on the other vessel had been extinguished, but he was not alerted by this as it was a common practice on passenger ships. Later white rockets were seen from the bridge by Second Officer Stone.

Fifty eight miles away, the wireless operator of the Cunarder *Carpathia* was shocked to receive *Titanic*'s distress call, 'Come at Once. We have struck a berg.' It returned the welcome message that they were 'coming hard', while two other vessels, the *Frankfort* and *Titanic*'s sister ship, *Olympic*, were also contacted. Coincidentally, the captain of the *Carpathia* was also a Bolton man – Arthur Rostron.

There were sixteen wooden lifeboats on *Titanic*, which if fully loaded could only carry about half the people on board. At 00.45 the first of these was lowered, being reserved for woman and children. At first many of the passengers were reluctant to leave the warmth of the luxurious 'unsinkable' liner, believing it was safer to stay aboard, but as the danger became more apparent, a terrible feeling of anguish swept through the ship as husbands and wives, children and fathers, were about to be parted from each other. In the space of an hour the light-hearted, carefree atmosphere had been transformed to one of stark horror. At five minutes past two the last of the lifeboats was lowered, leaving those who remained on board hoping for a miracle. Captain Smith told his crew, "Now it's every man for himself."

What must have seemed one of the most unreal aspects of the disaster was the way the 'best band on the Atlantic' continued filling *Titanic* with music, right to the very end. Of the eight musicians whose sound of ragtime was played to keep the spirits high, two were Lancastrians. Fred Clarke, a bass player from Liverpool, was making his first voyage, having left the Scottish concert circuit, but the band leader, Wallace Hartley from Colne, was an experienced ship's musician, having been lured from the *Mauritania*. The son of a choirmaster, Hartley had lived with music since childhood. He had given solo violin performances at the age of 15, then went on to become an orchestra leader in Bridlington. His dark, handsome appearance and engaging personality made him a popular figure when he later joined the sumptuous Curnard liners on which he had made eighty voyages across the Atlantic.

In her terrible death throes *Titanic* stood perpendicular from the icy sea. Then at twenty minutes past two, watched with fascinated horror by those lucky enough to have secured a place in her lifeboats, she slid slowly beneath the waves. It is said that Wallace Hartley's band were appropriately playing the hymn *Nearer My God to Thee*. Just ten miles away an officer aboard *Californian* saw the strange ship disappear, unaware that she had sunk, but it was 4.10am before the *Carpathia* arrived at the scene to begin to pick up the survivors.

Although the figures vary, it seems that about 1503 people lost their lives and 705 survived. The body of band-leader Wallace Hartley was found in the sea two weeks after the disaster, still dressed in his bandsman's uniform. It was brought back to Colne where 40 000 people, in poignant silence, watched his funeral cortège wind its way through the streets to the local cemetery. His gravestone bears the epitaph 'Nearer My God to Thee' and in 1915 his statue, paid for by public subscription, was erected in the town centre. The role which Boltonian Stanley Lord, captain of the *Californian*, played in the *Titanic* disaster became much more controversial. Why his ship failed to answer eight distress rockets from the stricken vessel has occupied historians ever since.

Although over eighty years have past since the tragedy, the interest in *Titanic* remains as strong as ever. Over 150 books, 17 films and 18 documentaries have covered every aspect of the disaster, museum exhibitions containing items retrieved from the wreck are planned and the British Titanic Society has an increasing membership.

Bandmaster Wallace Hartley, who perished aboard the Titanic, is buried at Colne

Loss of HMS Thetis

Lancashire has been associated with the Royal Navy Submarine Service since its beginning in 1901. It was the First Lord of the Admiralty, Lord Selborne, who announced to Parliament that the service was to be formed and that five submarine vessels of a type invented by John P. Holland were to be built. Vickers shipbuilders at Barrow-in-Furness were chosen to construct these very first Hollands, and since that time have continued as prime builders of submarines.

When Submarine Number 1 was launched on the 2 October 1901, it was a milestone in our naval history, but it soon became apparent that submariners needed to possess special qualities to cope with the difficult conditions found aboard these boats. Life could be extremely hazardous working in a confined space, the interior of the vessels being dark, noisy and smelling of engine oil. Lancashire, and particularly Liverpool with its seafaring tradition, produced many of these 'submarine types'; men who had both the skill, stamina and placid nature to live cheerfully beneath the waves.

Over the next four decades the development of submarines advanced beyond all early expectations and they became an extremely important and reliable part of the naval deterrent. So it was with quiet confidence that Lieutenant-Commander Guy Bolus took his brand new submarine *Thetis* out of Cammel Laird shipyard at Birkenhead on the 1 June 1939. She was bound for Liverpool Bay to begin her first diving trials.

The new 'T' class submarine had a crew of 53, but for this first trial another 50 personnel were also aboard, being mainly engineers and workmen from Merseyside together with some Royal Navy observers. Accompanied by the Liverpool tug *Grebecock*, she set course for a position 15 miles north of Llandudno off the Welsh coast.

The order to dive was given at 1400 hours, the vents being opened and the main ballast tanks flooded, but *Thetis* refused to submerge. The auxiliary ballast tanks, usually used only to balance a vessel, were also flooded, yet again she failed to drop beneath the water. It was becoming apparent that she had probably been made too light, but it was necessary to check that all the tanks were indeed full of water. The Torpedo Officer then began to inspect all the six bow torpedo tubes, which surprisingly seemed to be empty. Tube number 5, also appeared to have no water inside, but when the door was being opened for visual inspection it began to give out a spray. Suddenly the pressure became so great that it forced the tube door fully open and the whole torpedo compartment began to fill with water, causing the vessel to dive. Soon her bows were touching the muddy sea bed in 160 feet of water.

Lieutenant Coltart who was aboard the observer tug had witnessed the initial diving problems of *Thetis* and was a little uneasy at the way she had finally submerged, but not wishing to cause unnecessary alarm, he waited two hours before contacting the naval base at Gosport by telegram. Unfortunately, the telegraph boy at Gosport Post Office had a puncture in his bicycle tyre which further delayed the relaying of the message so the crew and engineers of *Thetis* had been struggling with their ordeal for two and a half hours before alarm bells began to ring ashore.

An immediate rescue operation was organised, the destroyer *Brazen* sped to the scene and six Ansons, based in Scotland, began to search the area. *Grebecock* had, however, drifted several miles from the dive position and darkness was quickly falling so it was 0754 the following morning before the sub was at last located, and by this time her stern was protruding high out of the water.

With only six hours of air remaining, conditions aboard were becoming desperate, every move requiring an almighty effort. Guy Bolus decided to 'escape' two knowledgeable officers to the surface to explain the position, and these were followed by two other men. The whole country had by this time heard of the intense drama that was unfolding so close to home.

The Liverpool salvage vessel *Vigilant* was used to secure wires around *Thetis* to ensure she did not slip further into the water as the rescue attempt continued. At first hopes were high, for it seemed unthinkable that a submarine partly visible above the water could be in such danger. Covers were removed from the stricken vessel and oxy-acetylene equipment arrived which was to be used to cut a hole in her stern. Frantic efforts were made to raise her further out of the water so that the work could be carried out, but then to the horror of the rescuers, the wire support broke. They watched helplessly as *Thetis* began to slip slowly beneath the sea; they knew the ninety-nine men aboard were now doomed.

The whole nation was stunned by the loss, it remains the worst submarine disaster in the United Kingdom. It took five months before she was raised then beached at Moelfre Bay, Anglesey. The bodies of the 99 men were removed and buried at Holyhead where she was dry docked.

Merseyside later witnessed the sad spectacle of *Thetis*, under her own power, arriving back at the shipyard where she had been built. At first it was intended that she would be dismantled, but by this time the war had begun, making every single vessel important. So instead she was re-commissioned, taking the new name of *Thunderbolt*, but in view of her recent history, any member of the drafted ship's company was allowed to request a transfer to another submarine if they wished.

Under the command of Lieutenant C.B. Crouch she again began acceptance trials in 1940, this time passing all the tests without a hitch. She then began a successful war patrol which took her into the Bay of Biscay, to Canada and into the Mediterranean. In March 1943 she left Malta, heading towards the coast of Sicily where she attacked a convoy of Italian ships. The corvette *Cicogna* was one of a number of Italian vessels which then began to hunt *Thunderbolt*. A loud echo finally gave away her position, then her periscope was spotted. Twenty-four depth charges were quickly hurled into the water and for the second time the Birkenhead built submarine was sunk and her crew lost.

Air Tragedies

Lancashire has been the scene of many tragic air crashes over the years, its cloud-covered moorland summits proving to be particularly hazardous for aircraft in trouble. Each year on Remembrance Sunday a poignant ceremony is held on a lonely high point on Anglezarke Moor near Chorley, to remember one of these. A stone memorial column carries the names of the crew of Zulu 8799, a Wellington Bomber which crashed on the 16th November 1943. The plane had taken off from Wymeswold in Leicestershire on a Bullseye Exercise. Its pilot was Flight Sergeant Joseph B. Timperon who came from faraway Alice Springs in Australia and was attached to the RAF from the Royal Australian Air Force. The other five crew members were Sergeants Eric Barnes, Joseph B. Hayton, Robert S. Jackson, Matthew Mouncy and George E. Murray.

As the aircraft flew low over upland Lancashire it began to get into difficulties, causing its engines to start screeching. The pilot, wrestling with the controls, failed to lift its great bulk above the peaty summit of Hurst Hill and it tore into the hillside. All the crew were killed, with wreckage being scattered over a large area. The RAF investigation which followed decided that the tragedy had most likely been caused by a 'loss of control in cloud, possibly due to icing' which may have led to structural failure as it went into a high speed dive.

Just a few miles away, on the high summit of Winter Hill on Rivington Moor, another terrible disaster occurred on Thursday the 27 November 1958. Heavy snow with drifting had blocked many roads on the West Pennine Moors at this time and visibility was down to about fifty metres. In these hazardous wintry conditions a Silver City Airways' Bristol 170 was on its approach to Manchester Airport from the Isle of Man. It was carrying a group of prominent businessmen from the island to a trade exhibition in the city.

The first indication that anything was wrong came when the staff of an isolated TV station which stands alongside a high mast close to the hill summit heard knocking on their door. They were amazed to find First Officer Howarth, bleeding from a head wound but fully conscious, shouting that his plane had crashed just a quarter of a mile away. The rescue services were immediately summoned, then the men from the TV station went out in the treacherous conditions, forming the first rescue party. Quickly news of the crash spread and many others risked their lives in the appalling weather to reach the site. Within two hours a special RAF Snowfly had cleared the road of the huge snow drifts, making it possible for a fleet of ambulances to get through. Helicopters had also been summoned from Anglesey and Yorkshire but due to the thick cloud were unable to land.

As the day wore on the true enormity of the crash became apparent. The dead bodies of thirty-four men were recovered and eight others escaped with injuries, but one of these died later. An inquest held in nearby Horwich

The Wellington Bomber Memorial on isolated Anglezarke Moor

found the disaster had been brought about by a succession of unfortunate incidents, but there had been no criminal negligence and a verdict of 'death by misadventure' was recorded. A memorial plaque has in recent years been placed on the side of the TV station, remembering those who lost their lives and the gallant efforts of the rescuers.

Another terrible Lancashire air crash that occurred during the last war still brings back tearful memories to the local villagers for it was made particularly horrific in that it resulted in the death of innocent children. Today many holidaymakers pass through the Fylde's largest village, Freckleton, on their way to sample the pleasures of Lytham or Blackpool. Most of these visitors are blissfully unaware that its sleepy rural face hides many a dramatic secret for during the Second World War this area was buzzing with activity. At nearby Warton was an airfield with the longest runway and the largest hangar in the whole of Europe. It was the main American airbase for the massive Liberator bombers and the whole area was alive with thousands of USAAF personnel.

Tragedy came suddenly one hot, thundery summer's day in August 1944 after one of the Liberators lifted off the runway like a giant bird. Having ascended into the ever-blackening sky, the pilot then decided the violent thunder that he suddenly met made it too risky to continue so he decided to return to the base. As he swooped low over Freckleton his machine touched the tops of some trees and immediately it plunged to the ground. Out of control, it ploughed directly into the village school in which the local children were busy at their lessons. Thirty-eight of the young pupils were killed and another twenty-three adults also died in what must rank as one of England's most horrific aviation disasters. The grim casualty list later revealed that two teachers, several villagers, the crew and six airmen who had been in a snack bar had died. Only three children from the infant's class had survived, in an instant Freckleton had lost a tenth of its population.

The horror of the event devastated the village at the time, and the loss of so many young people is still felt today. A procession of servicemen carried the tiny coffins of the children through the streets to their last resting place in the graveyard of Holy Trinity Church. A fine memorial now remembers those who died so young, and in 1977, aided by government grants, a Memorial Hall was built as a permanent reminder of the tragedy. Today the runway at Warton still echoes with the sound of aircraft for it is now part of the Military Aircraft Division of British Aerospace.

There have been numerous other military air crashes in Lancashire, and in some cases parts of the wreckage still remain hidden. Another Liberator crashed on Hameldon Hill in 1945, and following engine failure, a Blackburn Skua crashed near Higher Bentham in 1940, but the pilot was able to bale out. Three North American Mustangs crashed in separate incidents during the war near Rochdale, Clitheroe and on Darwen Moor, and a USAAF Thunderbolt from Burtonwood air base tragically tore into the side of Pendle Hill.

Fresh flowers mark the graves of those who died in the Freckleton air-crash

On the 8 May 1948 Battle of Britain veteran, 27-year-old Flying Officer Robert Hugh Price Griffiths of 611 Squadron took off in his Spitfire XIVe from RAF Woodvale near Southport. With the drama of the war now three years behind him, this training flight would have no doubt seemed to be merely routine. Sadly, this was not to be the case for as he soared to 21 000 feet above the Ribble estuary, he is believed to have suffered a failure in his oxygen system. With the pilot unconscious at the controls, his Spitfire plummeted helplessly to the ground.

The plane buried itself deep in the soft earth of a wheat field at Grange Farm on Freckleton Marsh, then exploded. Local people who rushed to the scene to help knew immediately that their efforts were in vain for they found a huge 20-feet-deep crater which was quickly filling up with a mixture of aviation fuel and water. Acrid fumes from the explosion also filled the air. An RAF salvage team who were soon at the site had the sad task of recovering the body of Flying Officer Griffiths. He was later buried with full military honours at St Peter's Church, Formby. The accessible wreckage of the aircraft was removed from the field by the RAF and the crater filled in. Soon the unfortunate incident was almost forgotten.

But nearly half a century later, in 1996, with interest in the epic era of the Spitfire growing, the site of the crash has been rediscovered. Members of the Pennine Aircraft Recovery Team, using a highly sensitive metal detector known as a magnetometer, after painstaking efforts finally located the spot where the aircraft crashed. Appropriately on Remembrance Sunday they started a dig which it is hoped will eventually lead to the recovery of the Spitfire's powerful Rolls Royce Griffin engine, which it is believed still remains on the site. This will then be displayed in one of Lancashire's museums.

The Munich Air Disaster

To millions of people around the world, Lancashire is now known for just one thing, it is the home of Manchester United! You may either love or loathe football, yet you cannot ignore it. Each year the sport generates hundreds of millions of pounds, employs thousands, and this single glamour club probably brings more positive publicity to the region than any other source.

The present outstanding success of Manchester United can be traced back to 1945 when a new manager named Matt Busby took control. He was a quietly spoken Scotsman who had ended a brilliant career in which he had played for both Liverpool and Manchester City. He proved to be an even greater club leader for during the next decade he transformed what had been an unpredictable team into the best in England. His players, who because of their youth were termed the Busby Babes, rose to ever greater success. During the next decade they won the FA Cup, became League Champions three times, and began to gain an enviable international reputation.

So it was in this climate of optimism during the 1957-58 season that the players were fighting to carry off the European Cup. Led by their Manchester-born captain, Roger Byrne, the celebrated team consisted of: Duncan Edwards, David Pegg, Mark Jones, Eddie Colman, Bill Foulkes, Tommy Taylor, Jackie Blanchflower, Geoff Bent, Bill Whelan, Bobby Charlton, Dennis Viollet and goalkeeper, Harry Gregg. They had played the first leg of the quarter finals in Manchester on the 14 January 1958 against the Yugoslav team, Red Star, and won by 2 goals to 1. In February they then flew out to Belgrade for the second leg. In wintry conditions, a tough match followed which ended in a draw. Triumphant Manchester United had won on aggregate so once more they had secured a place in the semi-finals.

On the morning of 6 February, the players, team officials and press representatives arrived at Belgrade airport for the flight home. Their plane, a BEA Elizabethan, had ex-RAF pilot Captain James Thain in command, aided by his First Officer Kenneth Rayment. They took off into the wintry sky, setting a course for Munich where a refuelling stop was scheduled. Here they arrived at 13.11, having descended through thick cloud onto a slush-covered runway.

The passengers had less than an hour in which to stretch their legs and buy their duty-free goods before returning to the aircraft for the final flight home. At 14.30 clearance for take-off was given, but at the last minute, after full power had been reached, Rayment suddenly abandoned take-off. He had heard an uneven sound from the engine which worried him. However, this power-surging was not uncommon, so at 14.34 take-off was again attempted, the pilots hoping that slowly opening the throttle would solve the problem. The fault occurred again and Thain this time abandoned take-off.

All the passengers were then sent back to the airport lounge while the 'technical fault' was sorted out. The BEA Engineer explained to the pilots that the engine surging was probably due to the height above sea level of Munich Airport, so after a discussion it was decided to make a third take-off attempt. As the passengers were brought back to the aircraft, the pilots now talked about having the wings swept of snow, but decided this was not necessary.

At 14.56 permission was given to taxi out, then following the usual checks, the aircraft began its take-off from a runway piled high with slush. Initially everything appeared normal, then quite suddenly a lack of acceleration at the crucial moment became sickeningly apparent; the two flyers knew they were not going to make it. The plane tore through a fence, sped over a road, then hit a house. The impact ripped off a wing and a portion of the tail, causing the building to burst into flames. Still the aircraft slithered on, partially disintegrating as it hit a tree, then a lorry in a shed which also caught fire, before finally coming to a halt in a mass of flames.

In the smoky horror of tangled metal, 21 of the 44 people on board had died. These included seven players: Byrne, Colman, Pegg, Bent, Whelan, Taylor and Jones, together with three United officials and the legendary Frank Swift. Their manager, Matt Busby, lay seriously injured.

It was a stunned Manchester that received the terrible news, putting the city into a state of mourning. The whole world was shocked by the tragedy, with messages of sympathy flooding in from every corner. News from Munich not only told of the dead, but also of those who had suffered terrible injuries in the crash. Fractured skulls, broken limbs, internal injuries and shock had affected many. Matt Busby was so badly hurt that he was given the last rites, but miraculously he was destined to survive.

The following week the flag-draped coffins of the dead were brought home from Munich. Over 100 000 people lined the streets of Manchester, many in tears. And for the uninjured survivors who also arrived there was massive media attention, together with great public sympathy. The terrible effects of the disaster were not yet over, however. The seriously-injured 21-year-old Duncan Edwards, who had been the youngest player ever selected for the England team, later lost his brave fight for life.

The German Court of Inquiry into the accident decided that it had occurred because of a layer of ice that had formed on the wing, but after a ten-year struggle, Captain Thain, who disputed this decision, persuaded a British Inquiry that it had resulted from the effects of slush on the runway. However, the greatest triumph that evolved from this horrific tragedy is to be seen today in the name of Manchester United: from the apparent hopelessness of the decimated club of 1958 has grown the best in Britain.

Horror at Burnden Park

For Bolton Wanderers Football Club, 1997 was a momentous year. Not only did they gain promotion to the Premier League but they played their last match at Burnden Park before moving to a brand new stadium. Naturally this was a time to look back to the many great matches played at Burnden over the last century, when past heroes like Dick Pym and Nat Lofthouse thrilled the huge, cheering home crowd. However, one date is forever etched in the mind of older supporters, sadly not because of triumph but because of a tragedy which occurred on Saturday the 9th March 1946.

The day began full of optimism for many Bolton supporters: the sun was shinning brightly, springtime was fast approaching and just six months earlier the end of the Second World War had been officially declared. In this mood of excited anticipation the fans began to make their way up Manchester Road, intent on taking their places in the stands and on the terraces. The match they were about to watch was the crucial sixth round of the FA Cup against their strong opponents, Stoke. In the home team was Nat Lofthouse, a 20-year-old youth who had yet to achieve national fame, but Stoke possessed the greatest player of the period, Stanley Matthews, whose presence always drew in huge crowds.

By one o'clock all the entrance gates had been opened and the crowds of light-hearted supporters were flocking through. By 2.40pm the turnstiles to the Railway Embankment were closed by the police as the ground was now full. Officially 65 419 people had now filled Burnden Park, but about 15 000 disappointed fans still remained outside. Many resigned themselves to missing the game, but others were still determined to gain entrance. These fans climbed the embankment of the nearby railway then, after removing parts of the sleeper fence, joined the bulging crowd of 28 137 who were packed like sardines in that part of the ground.

With the excitement that prevailed at the start of the match the situation grew ever more desperate. The huge pressure of human bodies increased as more people continued to illegally enter the embankment. Finally the force grew so great that the barriers were flattened, rows of people being pushed helplessly forward, one on top of the other. Many spilled over onto the track around the touchline, but others were crushed underfoot by their fellow supporters who were unable to prevent themselves being carried forward in a great wave.

The match at this point was proceeding as normal, both the players and the rest of the supporters unaware that a tragedy was unfolding, but the police had realised that this was more than a mere overspill. As they quickly investigated, to their intense horror they discovered scores of casualties. Crushed bodies lay motionless on the edge of the field, many seriously injured and others obviously dead.

At twelve minutes past three the referee was told to stop the game, removing the players from the field. The terrible task of removing bodies was then rapidly undertaken, but still only those fans close to the embankment were aware of the true extent of the disaster. At 3.20pm the Chief Constable decided that to abandon the match with such a huge crowd present might result in even more tragedy from disappointed fans so after consultation with the referee, play was resumed.

Many of the estimated 85 000 crowd returned home after the match completely unaware of what had really taken place at Burnden Park that fateful day. Only later did they hear the horrific news: 33 people were dead and over 500 injured. Among those who lost their lives were a father and son, a brother and sister, and a 14-year old-boy from Blackburn.

An inquiry that followed decided that the number of fans officially allowed into the Embankment was 2000 too many for safety, the enclosure shape was partially to blame as it created a bottleneck, and the unauthorised entry of fans was also a factor.

In September 1992 a plaque, in remembrance of those who lost their lives was unveiled at the Embankment End of Burnden Park. Sir Stanley Matthews, Nat Lofthouse, and Mary Coward, whose husband died in the tragedy, were present. To mark the 50th anniversary in March 1996, prayers were offered at a memorial service held at Bolton parish church.

Weather Chaos

It was Lancashire's reputation for damp air which is said to have first attracted the cotton industry to the area, as this resulted in the thread being less likely to break during the weaving process. However, over the years the county has experienced much more than 'damp air', for force ten gales, deep floods, blinding blizzards and even the odd tornado have been recorded, sometimes causing turmoil and even death.

Lancashire's flat coastline, lacking the protection of high cliffs, has always been at the mercy of the raging sea. In the past, when a combination of high tides and heavy gales prevailed the land for miles inland became flooded for months. The villagers of Tarleton often went to church at Croston not by horse but by boat, for the two communities became islands at such times.

Sailors in their flimsy wooden ships were no match for these tempests, often being wrecked on sandbanks or blown ashore. In 1643, during the Civil War, a Spanish warship, whose crew had been hit by plague, got into difficulties near Rossall Point during a strong gale. Eventually, the crew managed to alert the local people who saved them, but then a battle to seize their cannon raged between the Roundheads and Cavaliers. The Earl of Derby was the first on the scene, ordering his men to set fire to the empty ship so that the guns would not fall into the Roundheads' hands. But after the Royalists had left their enemy was still able to drag the cannons ashore with ropes, then take them triumphantly to Lancaster Castle.

In January 1839 Lancashire was hit by a tremendous storm which battered the coast, causing a huge amount of damage to shipping. Fifteen fishing vessels from Lytham were sunk and the shore at Rossall was covered with tobacco from a London-based cargo ship which had been lost with all hands.

But it was the wreck of the *Crusader*, a 584-ton vessel bound for Bombay from Liverpool, which brought the most bounty to the villagers of the Fylde. It was wrecked off Blackpool, scattering its high value cargo of silk and cotton goods along the beach. Although its captain and crew had a lucky escape, little of its cargo was ever seen again. In a scene reminiscent of Comptom Mackenzie's *Whisky Galore*, the people of Marton descended on the shore and in a flash the goods had completely disappeared!

Close to the pier at St Anne's a poignant memorial showing the figure of a lifeboatman records one of England's worst lifeboat disasters. This happened on the 9th December 1886, when the iron barque *Mexico* left Liverpool in a rapidly worsening gale which blew it onto a sandbank near

Southport. Three lifeboats answered the distress call: the *Charles Biggs* from Lytham, the *Laura Janet* from St Anne's and the *Eliza Fernley* from Southport.

In the raging force seven the Lytham lifeboatmen carried out a magnificent rescue, but sadly their colleagues were not as fortunate. The *Eliza Fernley* was capsized by a massive wave which left only two of her crew alive, while the fate of the *Laura Janet* was never fully revealed for her entire crew tragically died.

Lancashire's July weather, although often hot and sunny, sometimes has a sting in its tail. This comes in the form of crashing thunder storms which, although short-lived, can bring with them a deluge of rain causing local flooding on the sun-hardened ground. But few can ever match that which occurred in Middleton in 1927 for it brought complete chaos to the town.

Lying in a valley to the north of Manchester, Middleton had always been vulnerable to flooding for three waterways converge in the centre of the town: the River Irk, the Wince Brook and the Whit Brook. These began to rise rapidly on the 11 July 1927 following a prolonged storm that showed no sign of abating. The sky, which was alive with deafening thunder and blinding lightening, had taken on a strange, reddish hue.

The final blow came when the massive build-up of water caused the embankment of the Rochdale Canal to collapse. Full to the brim, its waters then roared down to join the already swollen river, producing a huge torrent that was unstoppable. It tore into the town, carrying with it all kinds of debris and creating a sea of foul-smelling mud. The water swept across streets then, taking residents unaware, it poured through their homes, smashing doors and furniture. Escaping to the safety of their bedrooms, they could only stare in horror as their houses were destroyed. When the water level eventually fell, four hundred people found themselves homeless and three had lost their lives. But during the confusion and devastation others had been miraculously saved by the dramatic heroism of their neighbours.

The last few months of 1935 brought exceptionally wet weather to Lancashire, with severe flooding in the Rossendale Valley causing the Irwell to burst its banks. In July 1936 the Manchester to Bolton canal at Nob End near Little Lever also burst its banks in spectacular fashion. A huge landslide of rocks and mud tore down a hillside into the Irwell far below. A torrent of water followed, emptying the entire canal along its length from Bury to Bolton and leaving a barge marooned precariously on the edge of a deep precipice.

The isolated village of Wray, which lies to the east of Lancaster, came into unexpected national prominence in August 1967. Although it was the height of summer, the county was experiencing a period of very heavy rain and thunder storms. The Rossendale Valley, the Ribble Valley and the Forest of Bowland were the worst hit, with over four and a half inches of rain falling in just two hours.

At Wray the day had started hot and dry, but by lunchtime distant thunder could be heard then torrential rain followed. The little River Roeburn, which starts on the high Bowland Fells then flows through the village, began to rise quickly, watched by two anxious farmers. Suddenly they saw a massive bank of water whirling like a tidal wave down the valley. Tossing large trees like matchsticks in its path, it demolished a footbridge and in seconds their farmhouse was surrounded by the raging torrent.

With a frightening roar the unstoppable water reached the village, hitting two cottages which broke up under the impact and were swiftly carried away. Heavy debris pounded other houses, crashing through masonry, breaking windows and sweeping away household goods. When the water level eventually subsided, miraculously there had been no deaths, but Wray would never be quite the same again. The great flood of 1967 has now become part of local folklore, the water level being indicated by a mark on the side of a bus shelter in the Main Street.

The Abbeystead Disaster

St Michael's-on-Wyre is one of Lancashire's prettiest villages, lying as it does in rural tranquillity midway between Lancaster and Preston. The church from which the village was named can trace its roots back to the 7th century, and was later mentioned in the Domesday Book. Its grey walls rise in ancient splendour, overlooking the gently flowing waters of the River Wyre. But inside the building a shining brass plaque on the wall stands as a poignant memorial to a recent tragedy from which the community is only just recovering: the Abbeystead Disaster.

It happened on the 23rd May 1984 when a party of villagers were on a visit to the Abbeystead water pumping station which had been constructed on the river about 12 miles upstream. The tour had been arranged to show them around the new installation which would end the threat of flooding in the village.

It was when a group of 44 visitors had gathered in the valvehouse to watch a demonstration of the new equipment that disaster struck. Unknown to anyone a huge pocket of methane gas had built up in an underground tunnel, then seeped into the area where the visitors were standing. Suddenly it was accidentally ignited, which led to an enormous explosion that tore through the concrete structure. Heavy beams collapsed on the helpless villagers causing some people to fall into the darkness far below.

News of the tragedy was flashed onto nationwide television as the rescue services rushed to the isolated location. As the hours past it became apparent that many were beyond help, the final death toll rose to sixteen with 28 others being badly injured. Among these was a mother and son, a married couple, and the wife of the headmaster from the village school.

The small community of 600 was stunned by the disaster which had shattered their lives. For weeks the village became the centre of media attention and only slowly did it return to some form of normality. Later came the fight for compensation for the survivors; a campaign which, helped by national press coverage, only ended when it reached the House of Lords.

It was decided that the 16 who died would be remembered by a simple memorial plaque in the village church which carries the message: 'Blessed are the dead who die in the Lord'. One of those who lost his life was engineer Geoffrey Seed who, as an employee of the water company, was showing the group around the pumping station. He was the husband of local cancer sufferer Pat Seed, whose amazing appeal fund raised £3.35 million for Christie's Hospital during her lifetime.

It is believed that the shock of losing her husband in the disaster led to her death just ten weeks later. However, her unique enthusiasm and inspiration continued to inspire and in 1997 the Pat Seed Appeal Fund reached its 20th anniversary, having now raised £7.5 million. A special celebration service was held in St Thomas's Church at Garstang where Pat once worshipped.

Chapter Ten

Curiosities

Prospect Towers

During the 12th century, when the raids of the Scots became a grave threat to the inhabitants of Lancashire, our windswept hilltops began to take on an added significance. By lighting huge fires on their summits the message of approaching danger could be quickly communicated to a large part of the county. First created by the Earl of Chester in 1138, these watch-fires or beacons were sited in a huge chain, visible from one to another. The warning could be sent over a distance of sixty miles in eleven minutes, allowing Lancastrians to take refuge in thick-walled Pele Towers, safe from the callous raiders.

The fires themselves were built from huge piles of wood that sat on a bed of stone on the top of the hill. However, in later years some beacons were housed in a special raised platform of iron supported on stout oak posts, barrels of tar being used as fuel. Over thirty of these beacons were scattered throughout the county, lighting up such prominent summits as Rivington Pike, Pendle Hill, Thieveley Pike, Boulsworth Hill, Warton Crag, and Blackstone Edge. Over the centuries their orange flames told of the rebellion against Henry VIII known as the Pilgrimage of Grace, the approach of the Spanish Armada, the Napoleonic Wars, and in more recent times they commemorated Queen Victoria's Diamond Jubilee and the coronation of King George V.

Some of the fine vantage points used as beacon sites began to be exploited in another manner during the 18th century when a series of prospect towers were constructed. Always of an ornate and highly individual design, they continued to be erected up to the end of the last century, often commemorating historic milestones of the period. Dominating the skyline of many Lancashire towns, each of these unique landmarks has its own colourful tale to tell.

The West Pennine Moors boasts three such towers, which linked together have become the basis of the popular Three Towers Walk. Rivington Pike Tower, perched on the rounded summit of this famous hill, is the oldest, having been built in 1733 by John Andrews. He had it erected to announce to the world that he was now the holder of the complete Manor of Rivington, which previously had been in two parts. Measuring 5.2 metres (17ft) square by 6.1metres (20ft) high, it was built at a cost of £85 3shillings using stone taken from the earlier beacon platform. Originally the castellated structure had windows, a door, a cellar and a fireplace and was used as a welcome refuge for grouse shooting parties. Today the doors and windows have been bricked up, but the tower remains as an impressive landmark which attracts many visitors. Once threatened with demolition, it is now protected as a Grade Two listed building.

Darwen Tower, the second of the trio, overlooks the towns of Darwen and Blackburn from a high point on the edge of Darwen Moor. This impressive structure was erected in 1897 to commemorate two events: the Diamond Jubilee of the reign of Queen Victoria and a local victory in a battle which had been fought to allow public access to the moors. Octagonal in shape, an in-

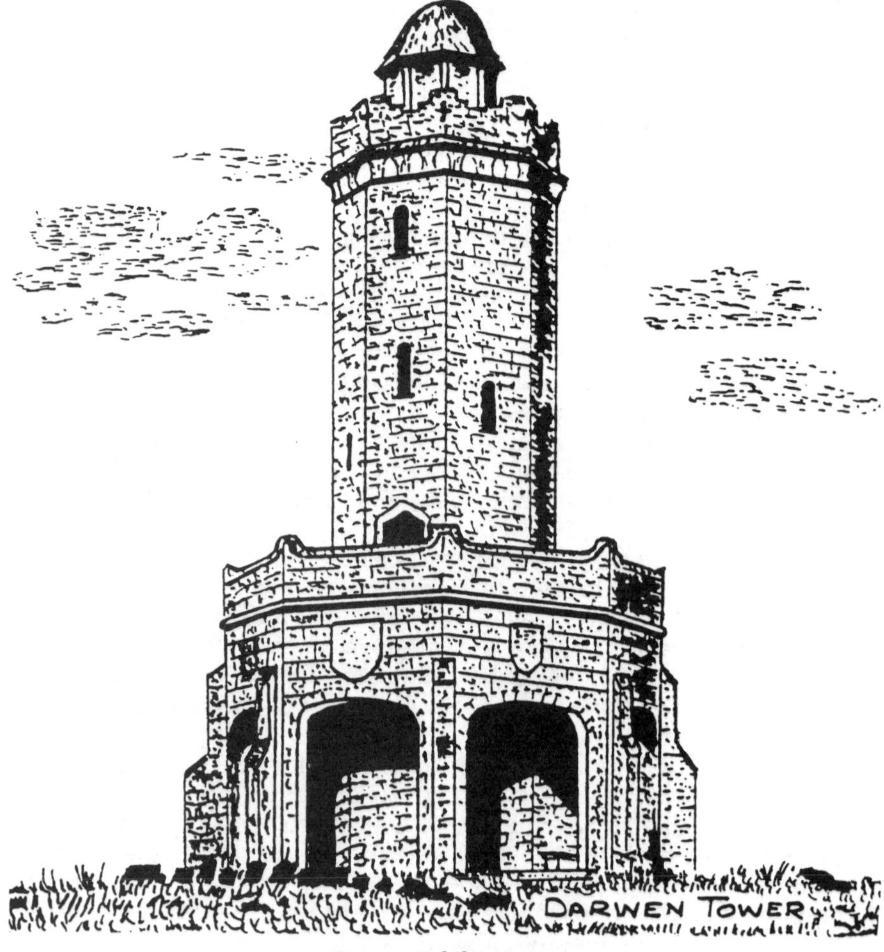

Darwen Jubilee Tower

ternal spiral staircase leads to two galleries which unveil a panorama that sweeps from the Peak District to Yorkshire. The landmark has another claim to fame for it was the first hill that Blackburn-born Alfred Wainwright climbed as a child. Perhaps motivated by the wildness of this landscape he went on to produce his classic pictorial guide to the Lakeland Mountains.

The dark finger of the Peel Monument on Holcombe Moor completes the Three Towers. Proudly standing sentinel over Rossendale, this 39metre (128ft) high structure was built in 1852 to commemorate the life of Sir Robert Peel. A handsome man of unusual intellect, he was born in nearby Bury in 1758. Rising to become a great Victorian Prime Minister, he founded the modern police force; the terms Peelers and Bobbies evolving from his name. It was his repeal of the much-detested Corn Laws which made food prices artificially high which gave him the greatest popularity among working class people. Originally costing £1000, the tower fell into disrepair this century so for safety reasons the entrance was bricked up. However, after restoration in 1985 it was re-opened to the public, who at weekends and bank holidays puff their way up the 157 steps to be rewarded by a marvellous view of East Lancashire.

Another series of three monuments which lie in West Lancashire can also be visited on a full day walk, beginning at Croston and ending at Billinge. The first one to be reached is the Bottle Beacon which stands close to the steep road which ascends Parbold Hill. This small, stone-built structure which stands about 2 metres high, gained its name from its curious bottle shape. It was constructed to commemorate the passing of the Reform Bill of 1832 and was restored in 1958. Although almost forgotten today, the passing of this Bill was a milestone in the democratic reforming process of the last century. It changed the electoral system, giving highly-populated commercial areas like Lancashire more seats in Parliament and the country districts less representation. This acknowledged that Britain was changing from an agricultural nation to an industrial nation.

Two miles from Parbold Hill, beyond the meandering path of the River Douglas, rises Ashurst Hill on which stands the second landmark of Ashurst Beacon. This is a square, stone structure surmounted by a tapering pyramid-shaped tower. Perched on a larger base reached by steps, the door and windows have been bricked up but it still provides a magnificent vantage point. The tower was first erected on this ancient beacon site by Lord Skelmersdale in 1798, the year Nelson gained his famous victory at the Battle of the Nile. A plaque relates how Mrs Florence Meadows presented the tower and its surrounding land to the people of Wigan in 1962 in memory of her journalist husband, Thomas Meadows.

Billinge Beacon, which stands on the summit of Billinge Hill, completes the West Lancashire trio of towers. Sadly neglected over the years, this folly now remains little more than a rather ugly, square, stone structure. It was first built on this prominent beacon site by the family who lived at nearby Winstanley Hall. Serving as both a summer house and a useful landmark for ships entering Liverpool bay, it remains a popular attraction for visitors because of the panoramic view obtained from the high point.

Lying three miles south-east of Oldham, Hartside Pike is a prominent high point on the foothills of the rising Pennines. The present 25.9metres (85ft) high circular tower with its tapering conical roof, stands at the summit of the hill on a site which has many historical connections. It is likely that a tower was in existence here at the beginning of the 18th century, then rebuilt in 1751. A century later this had become a sad ruin, but in 1863 the present impressive structure took its place. The project provided much needed work for unemployed men who were suffering because of the cotton famine brought about by the American Civil War. Built by public subscription, the tower commemorates the marriage of the Prince of Wales, later King Edward VII, to Princess Alexandra of Denmark, which took place in St George's Chapel at Windsor.

Looking towards the towering heights of Pendle Hill, Blacko Tower stands in countryside rich in pagan traditions. It was an eccentric grocer named Jonathan Stansfield who built this circular structure in 1891. From the top he hoped to see the home of his girlfriend at Gisburn, but unfortunately this proved impossible for the high ridge of Weets Hill blocked his view!

The Golden Jubilee of Queen Victoria was a perfect excuse to build all types of commemorative monuments. One of these lies close to the tortuous Trough of Bowland road which links Lancaster to the Ribble Valley at Quernmore. A square, castellated stone building, with a top reached by an outside flight of steps, this tower provides stunning views of the Lancashire coast. It was built in 1887 by James Harrison, a local man who had made a large fortune in shipbuilding. Another Jubilee monument of 1887 stands just six miles away on the marvellously named hill of Nicky Nook near Scorton. Similar to Parbold's Bottle Beacon in shape, this solid stone landmark looks down on the whirling traffic of the M6. Further north, Silverdale hides its Jubilee monument high on a limestone crag in thick woodland. Known as the Pepperpot due to its shape, this circular tower with a conical roof is a landmark popular with walkers. It was built by the local Hebden family in 1887 on the hill summit of Castlebarrow which they owned.

Of course, England's most famous prospect tower stands not on the summit of a hill, but soars proudly skywards from the Lancashire coast. For four generations Blackpool Tower has seductively tempted visitors to taste the delights of the glitter capital of Europe. Rising to a height of 158.4 metres (520ft) above the choppy Irish Sea, this delightful monster has become synonymous with our premier resort.

It was a former Mayor of Blackpool, John Bickerstaffe, who first put forward the idea of building the tower. About 1880 he had visited Paris where, like all visitors at the time, he had stared in wonder at the newly built Eiffel Tower. Back home he gathered together a group of business men, putting forward a proposal to give Blackpool a similar structure. This led to the formation of the Blackpool Tower Company which chose architects Maxwell and Tuke to produce the design. In September 1891 the foundation stone was laid, then less than three years later in May 1894, the magnificent tower was officially opened. With its superb ballroom, circus, restaurants and breezy viewing platforms, it remains our most enchanting folly.

Fylde Windmills

Windmills remain one of the most attractive man-made features of our countryside, dominating the landscape with their white towers and huge sails. In the Fylde we are particularly fortunate in having around a dozen of these fine structures still remaining, some having been restored to their former glory while others have been become private houses. Last century there were many more of these whirling giants, for it seemed that one stood on every high point. This led Bolton-born author Allen Clarke to give the title *Windmill Land* (1916) to his book which explored the splendour of this rural area.

Ancient man learned the essential art of grinding cereal between two stones to produce flour in pre-historic times. It was a process which led over many centuries to the development of the windmill. Its function was to harness the wind as a means of power, replacing, through a series of clever mechanisms, the need for hard manual work. They were known to be in use in Lancashire in the 13th century, at this time normally being under the control of the local Lord of the Manor.

To function efficiently the sails of the windmill cannot be in a fixed position, but need to be movable to accommodate the ever-changing wind direction. In the early wooden post-mills this was accomplished by revolving the whole body of the mill manually, using a tail-pole lever. In the later tower-mills, which can now be seen in the Fylde, only the sails and cap move. This is achieved automatically by having a controlling fan-tail which is fixed to the outside of the cap. It lies exactly opposite to the sails, which always turn in an anti-clockwise direction.

An interesting half-day can be spent, by car or cycle, discovering the remaining windmills of the Fylde. These are indicated on the Ordnance Survey Landranger Map, Sheet 102. A good starting point is Lytham's famous windmill which stands on the green overlooking the sea, and has become the symbol of the town (SD 370270). Now restored, it occupies the oldest remaining mill site in Lancashire for a mill has existed here for 800 years. The present structure was built in 1805, but following a disastrous fire was rebuilt in 1921. In 1909 a tragic accident happened when a young boy grabbed the turning sails which quickly carried him upwards. He then lost his hold, falling to his death.

Following the A584 through Freckleton, the next mill is reached at rural

Clifton (SD 464313), standing near a crossroads close to a wayside cross. When Allen Clarke came here eighty years ago he spoke to the miller who said it was at least 250-years-old. I visited this same mill almost thirty years ago, when it stood forlornly idle with one tattered sail, but now it has found a surprising new life as the Windmill Tavern! The tower has been tastefully incorporated into the main body of the pub, providing a unique drinking opportunity.

The next three windmills lie within four miles of each other and have all become private houses. Treales Mill (SD 446328), with its gleaming white tower, stands close to a country lane, among trees. Kirkham Mill (SD 431320), which twenty-five years ago was an empty shell and could boast to have been used as a lookout post during the Civil War, is now part of a residence named Wynde Milne. Similarly, Wrea Green Mill (SD 394315), which hides up a lane close to the neat green, had gaping holes and was roofless. It had been working with sails in 1770, then in 1860 its mechanism was converted to steam power, but sadly a boiler explosion brought its working life to an end. Today, with its pale yellow tower, it has become a pristine residence called The Old Mill House.

Marton Windmill (SD 348341) which stands alongside the busy A583 on the edge of Blackpool is a familiar sight to approaching holidaymakers. Perched on neatly trimmed grass, it has been carefully restored, being complete with sails and fan-tail. Appropriately, it stands as a memorial to Allen Clarke who was the much revered authority on Windmill Land.

Less than three miles away is the privately owned Staining Windmill (SD 346367), which lies on the edge of Staining village at the junction of Mill Lane and Smithy Lane, close to the line of a Roman road. Surrounded by pleasant meadows, the four-storey windmill is complete with sails, having been renovated following a fire. The village, which was mentioned in the Domesday book, is known to have had a windmill as early as 1529 which was probably on this same site. Uniquely in the Fylde, it possessed canvas covered sails instead of the more usual wooden slats.

Marsh Mill (SD 335426) at Thornton, which lies less than two miles from the sea at Cleveleys, has been transformed in recent years. Standing 21.3metres (70ft) high, it is the tallest Fylde mill, and was originally built in 1794 by Bold Fleetwood Hesketh who was the local Lord of the Manor. A later member of the family, Sir Peter Hesketh-Fleetwood, founded the new town of Fleetwood, which led to his bankruptcy. After he died, the mill and lands were bought by the Fleetwood Estate Company in 1875.

In 1896 the mill was modernised, then continued to operate until 1922, producing mainly animal feed. After being empty for six years it then found a new use and was converted into a café. In 1930 a tragic accident occurred when two women who were considering buying the mill fell to their deaths from the fan-tail platform.

During the next three decades it served as a storeroom, with the adjacent kiln-house becoming a private dwelling, until 1957 when it was bought by

Marton Windmill near Blackpool

the local District Council. Wyre Borough Council took over ownership in 1974, then followed a proposal in 1988 to make the mill the centrepiece of a tourist village. The mill was painstakingly restored with a pub, craft shops and some private flats being built nearby. On the 16 January 1990, in an atmosphere of excited anticipation, the crowds watched as the sails of the 196-year-old windmill began to turn once more. The mill now contains a tourist information centre and exhibition room where visitors can take a guided tour to the upper storeys.

Preesall Mill (SD 367467) lies off the narrow B5377 which leads to Knott End-on-Sea. Just its tower remains, without cap or sails, having found a new use as a glazing workshop. A post-mill existed in the village until 1839 when it was destroyed by a terrible storm which brought havoc to the Lancashire coast. Its loss must have caused disbelief to the villagers for according to a popular local rhyme they hoped their windmill would stand forever:

On Preesall Hill stands Preesall Mill,
As I've heard people say,
And if it does for ever stand,
It will forever stay.

However, within six months, with Victorian tenacity, construction of the present mill began. In its heyday it was as impressive as Marsh Mill, being of a similar height with six storeys, huge sails and a balcony.

The final windmill of the tour lies at Pilling (SD 407488), on the banks of a small river known as Pilling Water near Broadfleet Bridge. Now transformed into a private residence, it was built in 1808 by Ralph Slater, probably on the site of a watermill. Standing six storeys high, it entered a new era in the 1880s when it was converted to steam power; the cap and sails being removed. It continued to work for another forty years until its stones finally stopped grinding in 1926.

Church Oddities

The music of church bells echoing across the countryside is a sound which we have come to associate with peace and tranquillity. This has not always been the case for in the past, as well as calling the faithful to service, they were sometimes rung to drive away evil spirits when someone had died. At Downham, which is regarded by many as being Lancashire's prettiest village, the sound of bells from St Leonard's church has an unusual significance. When the bell was being recast in 1881, it was mixed with metal from the Great Paul bell from St Paul's Cathedral which was being recast at the same time so today there remains a little-known link between this country parish and Wren's great masterpiece in London.

At Whalley it seems that calendars were once in short supply for two gravestones in the churchyard bear the dates April 31st 1752 and February

30th 1819! The church also contains a brass memorial to Sir Ralph Catterall, his wife, and his twenty children. But his family was small compared to that of Sir Ralph Pudsey whose tomb at Bolton-by-Bowland is covered by a huge limestone slab. On it are carved his effigy, and those of his three wives and his twenty five children!

Warton Church near Carnforth can claim an important link with America's first president, George Washington, for it was his ancestor, Robert Washington, who built the church tower during the 15th century. Preserved inside is a carved stone containing his coat-of-arms of stars and stripes, which was adopted as the flag of the USA. To celebrate the connection, a large Stars and Stripes flag which once flew over the Capitol Building in Washington, is now flown from the church tower on the 4th July. It was at Chorley that Myles Standish, one of the original Pilgrim Fathers was born. He never forgot his birthplace of Duxbury Hall for he named his home in New England 'Duxbury'.

Bleasdale is an unspoilt rural area which lies beneath the rising Bowland Hills. Its small Victorian church is the only one in England to be dedicated to the little known Saint Eadnor. It is believed that this is a variation of the name Eadbert, who was the saint who followed the famous St Cuthbert at Holy Island then was buried in the same tomb.

At Winwick a pig has been sculptured on the church as a reminder of how the parish originated. It is said that when the first church was being built, the pig mysteriously appeared then proceeded to move the stones to the present site, which it had chosen. It even named the area by squeaking the word 'wee nick'! In the presbytery of St Mary's church at Hornby the shell of a tortoise named Moses is preserved. This was once the pet of the famous historian Dr Lingard, who was the parish priest for forty years.

The towering white steeple of St Walburge's church in Preston at 94.5 metres (310ft) high is the third tallest in England, being surpassed only by Norwich and Salisbury cathedrals. Its architect was Joseph Hansom who is remembered as the designer of the famous hansom cab. Ormskirk church, unusually, has both a steeple and a tower, the latter being built of stones taken from Burscough Priory to house the Priory's bells, while at Bradshaw near Bolton the church, which was re-built in 1872, has neither a tower nor steeple attached to it. However, standing apart from the building there remains a 15th-century tower which was part of the old church. It has also a rare dedication to Saint Maxentius who was a 6th century French monk.

Brindle Church, near Chorley, boasts five fonts which stretch back from the present day to the Norman Conquest, while St Stephen's church at Tockholes has a rare outdoor stone pulpit which was used for a service just once a year. Claughton in the Lune Valley can claim to have one of England's oldest, dated bells – it is inscribed 1296. The God Stone in Formby churchyard is a pre-Christian feature around which the tradition developed that every person being buried was first carried three times around the stone in the direction of the sun.

The secluded Roman Catholic church of St Anne, which lies at Sutton near St Helens, has become widely known as the Church of Three Saints. This is because the unlikely trio of a former aristocrat, an Italian peasant and a Shropshire girl are buried there, each one seeming to be destined for sainthood. These are Father Ignatius Spencer, great-great grand uncle of the late Diana, Princess of Wales; Blessed Dominic Barberi, a prospective Patron Saint of England; and Mother Joseph Prout, founder of the Sisters of the Cross and Passion.

Liverpool boasts the biggest Anglican Cathedral in the world. It took 74 years to build, being opened in 1978 by the Queen. Its architect was Sir Giles Scott who was a Roman Catholic. Appropriately, the nearby Roman Catholic Metropolitan Cathedral of Christ the King which opened in 1967 was designed by Sir Frederick Gibberd, a Protestant! But older than both of these is the little known Greek Orthodox Church which was authorised by the Czar of Russia in the 1860s.

Tunstall Church in the Lune Valley was immortalised by Charlotte Brontë when she renamed it Brocklebridge Church in *Jane Eyre*. It is said that in 1834 the young Brontë sisters, Maria, Elizabeth, Charlotte and Emily, ate their dinner on Sundays in a room over the church porch. At this time they were unhappy pupils at a school at nearby Cowan Bridge.

A Thankful Village

Arkholme is a tranquil village which hides down a quiet lane on the banks of the River Lune. It boasts many picturesque cottages, a fine 15th-century church, and a small green mound which many believe was built by Saxon hands. Its claim to fame, however, dates not in this legacy from the distant past, but from the First World War when it became Lancashire's only Thankful Village.

When hostilities came to an end on the eleventh hour of the eleventh month of 1918, England could never return to its pre-war condition for the horrors of Ypres, Gallipoli and scores of other battlefields had brought a carnage that affected nearly every family in the land. Tens of thousands of young men who had willingly left home to fight for our freedom had been dreadfully slaughtered in the mud of the trenches. The cream of a whole generation had tragically disappeared, leaving a terrible void. Bury was one of the worst hit towns in England, being the home of the Lancashire Fusiliers, for it had lost over 13 000 men. While the 700-strong Accrington Pals had 235 men killed and 350 wounded in one terrible misjudged advance at the Somme.

Miraculously, there were a handful of communities in England which had remained untouched by the hand of death, every single man who had served in the war having returned home safely. In 1936 the popular writer

Arthur Mee, when researching his book *The Enchanted Land*, discovered 23 such places which he termed 'The Thankful Villages'. Since that time further research has revealed that the total is 36.

Arkholme heads this list, having sent 59 men to war out of a population of 300 people. They had all been born and bred in the village, but eight had emigrated to New Zealand. At the outbreak of the war these returned to fight for their country alongside their childhood friends, and all survived.

Who's Buried Where?

Anyone who wanders through a graveyard reading the moss-laden inscriptions cannot help but be intrigued by the stories they reveal. Tantalising clues such as 'Dunkirk Veteran', 'Drowned at Sea', or 'Died aged 102 years' allow us to speculate on the unknown lives of those that lie buried. Although many have had a life that is worthy of recording, it is often only the famous, the infamous and the eccentric who are remembered. Lancashire has, of course, produced many such people, but often they have found fame and a last resting place outside the county. Fortunately, others have been buried closer to home, allowing us the opportunity to visit their graves and perhaps dwell on their achievements.

When Wigan-born comedian George Formby died in March 1961 more than 100 000 people lined the streets of Warrington to pay their last respects. This highly talented man, who had made twenty-two films and risen to become Britain's highest paid entertainer, was much loved by his fellow Lancastrians. His last resting place can be seen in Warrington Cemetery marked by an ornate white gravestone. He was buried alongside his equally famous father.

In September 1979 the flags were flown at half mast in Rochdale, the whole town was in mourning after learning that Gracie Fields had died. This astonishing woman, who had risen from being a poor mill girl to become our very first superstar, had never forgotten her roots. Today she has many memorials in the town including the Gracie Fields Theatre, but her grave lies far from her birthplace. Following a simple burial service, which surprisingly had no music, she was laid to rest in a small graveyard on her beloved Isle of Capri.

Samuel Crompton, the Bolton-born inventor of the spinning mule which brought enormous profits to many Lancashire mill owners, died penniless and heartbroken in 1827. His grave can be seen in the shadow of Bolton parish church in Churchgate, with his statue in nearby Nelson Square. A similar fate was shared by the inventor of the weft fork, John Osbaldeston, who died in the workhouse in 1862, but a grave space was given to him in St Stephen's churchyard in Tockholes village. At Bury there is a memorial to John

George Formby's grave at Warrington

Samuel Crompton rests in peace in Bolton Parish churchyard

Kay who invented the flying shuttle, but he lies buried in an unknown grave in France.

John Byrom, who wrote the popular hymn *Christians Awake*, was buried in 1763 in the Byrom Chapel of Manchester Cathedral. Almost two centuries later another hymn writer, Francis Duckworth, was laid to rest in the churchyard of St Mary-the-Virgin at Gisburn. His gravestone is appropriately inscribed with part of his famous composition *Rimington*, which was named after his birthplace near Pendle Hill.

Edwin Waugh, the dialect poet who became known as the Lancashire Burns, is buried beside the church at Kersal in Manchester, while Manchester-born historical novelist William Harrison Ainsworth, who wrote the ever popular *The Lancashire Witches*, died in 1882 at Reigate and was buried at Kensal Green Cemetery in London.

Journalist and travel writer, H.V. Morton, who was born in 1892 at Ashton-under-Lyne, wrote such classics as *In Search of England* and *In the Steps of the Master*. He went to live in South Africa in 1948 and died there in 1979. His ashes were scattered at his farm in Cape Province. Howard Spring, who after working at the Manchester Guardian went on to become a best-selling writer, used his adopted Manchester as the setting for many of his novels. He retired to Cornwall where he died in 1965, being buried in the churchyard at Mylor. Both men were chosen to record the historic meeting between Churchill and Roosevelt aboard HMS *Prince of Wales* in 1941, remembered in Morton's book *Atlantic Meeting*.

The northern part of the traditional county of Lancashire has become the last resting place of many eminent incomers, lying as it does in Lakeland, but George Romney, the 18th-century portrait painter who is best known for his studies of the beautiful Lady Hamilton, was a local man. He returned home to die after an absence of 37 years, and was buried in the churchyard at Dalton-in-Furness in 1802.

In Coniston churchyard, beneath an ornate cross, lie the remains of philosopher and art critic John Ruskin. But only a memorial in the village remembers water speed ace Donald Campbell who was killed on the nearby lake in 1967 for his body was never recovered. A few miles away in the Rusland valley, in St Paul's churchyard, is the grave of Arthur Ransome who wrote *Swallows and Amazons*, while at nearby Finsthwaite is the last resting place of the mysterious Clementina Johannes Sobiesky Douglass, who some believe was a daughter of Bonnie Prince Charlie.

In 1943 the ashes of children's writer Beatrix Potter, whose parents came from a prosperous Lancashire cotton family, were scattered on the hills around Near Sawrey, and the ashes of the Blackburn-born author of the classic Lakeland mountain guides, Alfred Wainwright, were appropriately scattered near the remote Innominate Tarn above Buttermere in 1991.

In the village of Holme, near Burnley, can be seen the simple grave of General Scarlett, a hero of the Crimean War who rode at the head of the Heavy Brigade. However, the brilliant historian and priest John Lingard, lies not in his native Hornby where he served for 40 years, but at Ushaw in Durham.

Those who are seeking out the grave of the 17th-century Baptist preacher Roger Worthington, will find it not in a churchyard but in a field, for he asked to be buried in a quiet corner of Hawkshaw Village, near Bury, leaving money for the upkeep of the grave. The original gravestone was broken last century when a horse stumbled against it, but in 1934 the site was restored to coincide with the 225th anniversary of his death.

Another lonely grave is to be found at Sunderland Point, a narrow, tapering peninsula which lies at the estuary of the River Lune. In the corner of a green meadow, beneath a small white cross, Sambo is buried. He was a young, black cabin boy who was brought over to Lancashire by the captain of a sailing ship during the 17th century, then died. As he was not a Christian he was not allowed burial in consecrated ground. Surprisingly, two alleged witches were allowed to be buried in consecrated ground. In St Anne's churchyard at Woodplumpton, near Preston, a boulder marks the resting place of Meg Shelton who died in 1706. It is said she was buried upside down to prevent her escaping! A table tombstone alongside the south wall of St Mary's church at Newchurch in Pendle is traditionally known as the 'witches grave'.

Index

Also of interest:

JOURNEY THROUGH LAKELAND: the history, customs and beauty of the English Lake District

"...a most enjoyable diary, wide ranging in its coverage and appreciative in its comments" – THE KESWICK REMINDER. *£7.95*

JOURNEY THROUGH LANCASHIRE: the history, customs and beauty of Lancashire

"Packed with whimsy & wonder" – THIS ENGLAND. *£7.95*

TEA SHOP WALKS IN LANCASHIRE

Clive Price has devised the 30 walks in this book to explore the landscape of Lancashire, crossing high moorlands and following riverside paths. Lancashire is a county renowned for its hospitality and baking, so to round off each walk, there is a specially selected tea-room, where you can sample tea and freshly-baked scones - smothered in cream from the local cows! *£6.95*

All of our books are available from your local bookshop. In case of difficulty, or to obtain our complete catalogue, please contact:
Sigma Leisure, 1 South Oak Lane, Wilmslow, Cheshire SK9 6AR
Phone: 01625 – 531035
Fax: 01625 – 536800
E-mail: sigma.press@zetnet.co.uk
Web site: www.sigmapress.co.uk

ACCESS and VISA orders welcome – use our 24 hour Answerphone service! Most orders are despatched on the day we receive your order – you could be enjoying our books in just a couple of days. Please add £2 p&p to all orders.